"Hand to heaven, Pastor Mike's faith has not only inspired me, but it has transformed me. I've always considered myself a woman of faith, but this book (and Mike's life) has pushed me to dream bigger, believe for more, and possess crazy faith! The best part of crazy faith is that it transforms into contagious faith in which we cannot help but tell everyone about a *big* God who does *big* things and fulfills *big* dreams. This isn't something Mike just believes; this whole book is what he breathes."

—BIANCA JUAREZ OLTHOFF, author, podcaster, and co-pastor of the Father's House, Orange County

"𝕮𝖗𝖆𝖟𝖞 𝕱𝖆𝖎𝖙𝖍 is a beautifully inspiring, laugh-out-loud funny, and incredibly profound journey into the lifestyle of faith. Faith is so important to me because I believe it's how we honor God. I trust Mike's words in this book because he's walked this journey before writing about this journey. Lean in and get ready because you won't be the same after you read this book!"

—CHAD VEACH, lead pastor of Zoe Church, Los Angeles

"It's tempting to think that either you are born with lots of faith or you aren't, but that's not how it works! Faith is a muscle that can be strengthened as we walk with God, and even a mustard seed of faith can move mountains. In 𝕮𝖗𝖆𝖟𝖞 𝕱𝖆𝖎𝖙𝖍, Michael shows us exactly what that looks like, pointing to a crazy big God who will be there for you even when it seems impossible. Don't read this book if you are okay with where you are; it will spoil your appetite for the status quo."

—LEVI LUSKO, lead pastor of Fresh Life Church and bestselling author

Crazy Faith

MICHAEL TODD

Crazy Faith

IT'S ONLY CRAZY UNTIL IT HAPPENS

WATERBROOK

CRAZY FAITH

Details in some anecdotes and stories have been changed to protect the identities of the persons involved.

2023 WaterBrook Trade Paperback Edition

Images on page 10: iStock (adapted)

LIBRARY OF CONGRESS CATALOGING-IN-PUBLICATION DATA
Names: Todd, Michael (Pastor), author.
Title: Crazy faith : It's only crazy until it happens / by Michael Todd.
Description: Colorado Springs : WaterBrook, 2021. | Includes bibliographical references.
Identifiers: LCCN 2021021850 | ISBN 9780593239216 (trade paperback) |
ISBN 9780593239209 (ebook)
Subjects: LCSH: Christian life.
Classification: LCC BV4501.3 .T637 2021 | DDC 248.4— dc23
LC record available at https://lccn.loc.gov/2021021850

Printed in the United States of America on acid-free paper

waterbrookmultnomah.com

4 6 8 9 7 5 3

Most WaterBrook books are available at special quantity discounts for bulk purchase for premiums, fundraising, and corporate and educational needs by organizations, churches, and businesses. Special books or book excerpts also can be created to fit specific needs. For details, contact specialmarketscms@penguinrandomhouse.com.

To my only son, Michael Alexander Todd Jr.

You have given Daddy a reason to believe God in **𝕮𝖗𝖆𝖟𝖞 𝕱𝖆𝖎𝖙𝖍** that goes beyond my ability to express in words. I can't wait for us to have a conversation about how God did this miracle.

It's only crazy until it happens.

CONTENTS

———————

Crazy Faith

1

IT'S ONLY CRAZY
UNTIL IT HAPPENS

TODAY'S NORMAL WAS YESTERDAY'S CRAZY

Imagine with me that the year is 1979. I walk up to you, brimming with excitement, and announce that I have in my possession an electronic device that fits in the palm of your hand, with no cord or long antenna attached, that you can use to communicate with another person on the other side of the world. "I call it [pause for effect] . . . *a cell phone*!" You would probably think I need to be locked in a cell somewhere because clearly I am crazy.

Or let's say it's 1955, and racial tensions between Black and white people in America are sky-high. In some parts of the country, they're not even legally permitted to drink from the same water fountain. Imagine a young Black man walking up to a crowd of white people and declaring that his children and theirs will one day go into business together, attend the same church, and "maybe even [pause for effect] . . . *marry each other*!" That crowd wouldn't just think he was crazy but would probably go crazy *on* him, yelling racial slurs and possibly attempting to end his life.

How about we take it back a little further, to 1899. You're planning to visit relatives across the country for the holidays.

As you approach the train station for your weeklong journey, I show up and confidently inform you that in just four years, someone will create a prototype for air transportation. "It will be something like a giant metal bird that will take people wherever they want to go in a fraction of the time! And it will be called [pause for effect] . . . *an airplane*!" You would probably dismiss me as a nutcase before boarding your reliable and time-tested train, because you know such an idea is just plain crazy.

> ## SO MANY THINGS THAT SEEM NORMAL TODAY WERE CRAZY FIVE MINUTES AGO.

What if I told you that these little stories are based on actual events? There was a time when no one had ever imagined a cellular phone or racial integration or an airplane. A parking lot full of cars, the app you use to order your lunch delivery, women voting in elections, the chair you're sitting in, social media—all of these were once considered crazy . . . until they actually happened.

So many things that seem normal today were crazy five minutes ago. (Okay, sometimes more than five minutes. But a lot can change in a very short amount of time.) Once we recognize that, it's reasonable to acknowledge that many things that seem crazy to us right now could be normal in the future. Your student loan debt erased or your six-figure mortgage paid off seems crazy. Doctors going up to the ICU to tell the uncle you've been praying for that he's cancer free and can go home seems crazy. The thought of your entire family accepting salvation and living for Christ sounds crazy. Getting your ten-year sobriety chip after abusing substances for decades sounds crazy. Leaving an inheritance of wealth for your great-grandchildren after you grew up in poverty seems crazy. Recovering from what seems like an unending downward spiral of depression to wake up with real joy sounds crazy. Finding out your wife is twelve-weeks pregnant after a diagnosis of infertility seems crazy. Being the first in your family to graduate college when you're a single mom who barely finished high school seems crazy. Being truly loved in a healthy marriage after suffering years of verbal, physical, emotional, or sexual abuse sounds crazy. Forgiving your absent father sounds crazy. Leading a thriving megachurch with only six months of junior-college education sounds just plain crazy.

But it's only crazy until it happens.

You're reading this book because there is something in you that believes the impossible, that knows greater is inevitable, that trusts destiny is unavoidable, and that is intrigued by the possibility of a miracle. This is my life message because this is the life I'm living: one of **Crazy Faith**. God has asked me to do some crazy things, and I've seen crazy results because of faith. Through this book, I want to be your coach, your guide on this faith journey, by sharing spiritual truth and practical wisdom to help you gain new perspective on God's plans for you: a future you've barely dared to imagine.

Now, don't get it twisted; I haven't done everything perfectly. The Bible says the steps of a good man or woman are directed by the Lord (Psalm 37:23)—and let's just say, I've missed some steps. But

> I WHOLEHEARTEDLY BELIEVE THAT LIFE IS MORE ABOUT PROGRESSION THAN PERFECTION.

I've also learned *a lot* in the process. I wholeheartedly believe that life is more about progression than perfection, so let's be

H.O.T. (humble, open, and transparent) with each other and discover more of the great plan God has for us as we walk by faith.

But first, let's back up a little bit and get to know each other.

FOUNDATION OF FAITH

Hi! My name is Michael. I'm a devoted husband to Natalie Todd, my relationship goal, my baby mama, my boo, my good thang, the apple of my eye, the water to my thirst, the wife of my youth, the sweet to my sour that I need every hour . . . whew! Sorry, y'all, I got a little lost thinking about how fine she is. As a blessing of our love, we have four beautiful kids: Isabella Monet, who is her mother's little twin; MJ, whom I call my fearless hero; Ava Rae, who is a sassy thirty-year-old in a three-year-old's body; and our grand finale (fingers crossed), the newest addition to the #ToddSquad, Gia Simone. I'm an active father; lead pastor of Transformation Church, a ministry that impacts millions of people around the world (shout-out to TC Nation!); a CEO; a music producer; a designer; and—I don't know how this happened—a #1 *New York Times* bestselling author.

Wow. Writing all that feels crazy because at certain points in my life none of it seemed achievable.

Let me explain.

I grew up as one of five brothers in a strong faith-filled family. My parents are ministers who have always modeled a life of extreme faith for me. In moments when most parents would have said, "I'm sorry, we can't afford that right now," my mom told me to pray and believe God for what I wanted.

She and my dad told me Bible stories of extraordinary faith all the time, and I would imagine myself as one of the characters. It built in me much more than a good imagination; it built a solid faith foundation.

I'm fully aware that not all kids grow up like that, but the beautiful thing about faith is that it's never too late to build it. Sure, the best time to start laying that foundation may have been twenty years ago, but the next-best time is *right now*. In many translations, Hebrews 11:1 starts off with these two words: "Now faith." So I'm encouraging you now, at this moment, that now is not too late. As a matter of fact, now is the perfect time. Right where you are, you can begin tearing down the walls of doubt, pulling out the lies of pessimism, and removing the framework of fear so that God can pour a new faith foundation deep within you.

We each have beliefs, standards, philosophies, and habits, and these are all built on some sort of foundation, whether from family, friends, education, religion, or culture—or a combination of all of the above. I wrote this book to help you build a healthy, purpose-revealing, God-honoring life of faith, but before we start building anything, we need to establish some things on a ground level. Even the most glorious building can be reduced to a pile of rubble without a sure and solid foundation.

> THE BEAUTIFUL THING ABOUT FAITH IS THAT IT'S NEVER TOO LATE TO BUILD IT.

A foundation is essential to hold a structure in place, but it does so much more than that. A well-built foundation keeps out moisture, insulates against the cold, and resists shifting with the earth around it. It is strong, deep, and dense enough to last the lifetime of the building sitting on top of it. In the words of *This Old House* general contractor Tom Silva, "Without a good one, you're sunk."*

Over the past year, my wife and I have embarked on the relationship-testing journey of building a house, and we've learned a whole lot about construction and a whole lot about each other. (Y'all keep us in your prayers.) One of the things that has surprised us is how much intentionality goes into the planning, preparation, and configuration of the foundation: digging, measuring, steel reinforcing, cement mixing, leveling, and more. When I asked the foundation contractor why it was taking so long (because, honestly, I was ready to see some progress above ground), he reiterated that the foundation is the most important phase of construction. They never rush this part of the process because, as he put it in a very matter-of-fact tone, "We can fix a wall and we can repair a window, but once this house is up, the foundation is set forever—that is, unless we tear it down or do major reconstruction."

I couldn't help but wonder, *What areas of my life have I built on a faulty foundation? Where do I need some major reconstruction?*

Have you heard of the Burj Khalifa? No, it's not Wiz Khalifa's cousin. It's currently the world's tallest free-standing structure, at a staggering height of more than 2,700 feet— that's two and a half times as tall as the Eiffel Tower and almost twice as tall as the Empire State Building! It cost an estimated $1.5 billion and took six years to build.†

---

* Max Alexander, "All About Strong House Foundations," *This Old House*, www.thisoldhouse.com/foundations/21015176/from-the-ground-up -house-foundations.

† "Burj Khalifa Facts and Information," The Tower Info, https://thetower info.com/buildings-list/burj-khalifa.

More than 110,000 tons of concrete were used to construct the foundation, which is buried 164 feet below ground level. That's twelve stories of building *under* the building, because it takes a very deep, very sturdy foundation to keep that 500,000-ton tower standing tall.*

A foundation may seem insignificant because it's under the surface, but it makes possible the part that's on display for everyone to see. The integrity of the foundation you build your life on determines the type of structure that can be built on it. I am convinced that the foundation you should build your life on is faith in God and belief in His Word. God's Word has remained from generation to generation, has seen empires rise and fall, and produces change but will never change.

> THE INTEGRITY OF THE FOUNDATION YOU BUILD YOUR LIFE ON DETERMINES THE TYPE OF STRUCTURE THAT CAN BE BUILT ON IT.

> The grass withers and the flowers fade,
>   but the word of our God stands forever. (Isaiah 40:8)

Let's take a moment to assess our foundations together. Now, I need you to be H.O.T. (humble, open, and transparent). Which of the following best describes the kind of structure your current faith foundation can support?

The truth is, you can't build a skyscraper-sized vision on

---

* "Fact Sheet," At the Top: Burj Khalifa, www.burjkhalifa.ae/img/FACT -SHEET.pdf.

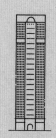

SKYSCRAPER

huge visions, giant goals, and daring dreams; lifestyle of faith on public display that is focused on serving countless others

MANSION

large, strong framework; intentionally designed to last a long time; aesthetically pleasing to attract others; set up to leave a legacy for future generations

FIXER-UPPER

pretty solid belief structure but compromised integrity due to doubt, disappointment, and damage over the years; needs some work

TRAILER HOME

not set in stone, easily moved, not anchored down; susceptible to damage from outside circumstances; doesn't have much room for others

PORTA-POTTY

used only as a last resort; usually full of crap; requires a lot of maintenance; has just enough room for one

VACANT LOT

no vision or direction; available; full of potential

FRIENDSHIPS

☐ SKYSCRAPER ☐ MANSION ☐ FIXER-UPPER ☐ TRAILER HOME ☐ PORTA-POTTY ☐ VACANT LOT

CAREER GOALS

☐ SKYSCRAPER ☐ MANSION ☐ FIXER-UPPER ☐ TRAILER HOME ☐ PORTA-POTTY ☐ VACANT LOT

ROMANTIC RELATIONSHIP

☐ SKYSCRAPER ☐ MANSION ☐ FIXER-UPPER ☐ TRAILER HOME ☐ PORTA-POTTY ☐ VACANT LOT

HEALTH
(MENTAL, EMOTIONAL, SPIRITUAL, PHYSICAL)

☐ SKYSCRAPER ☐ MANSION ☐ FIXER-UPPER ☐ TRAILER HOME ☐ PORTA-POTTY ☐ VACANT LOT

FINANCES

☐ SKYSCRAPER ☐ MANSION ☐ FIXER-UPPER ☐ TRAILER HOME ☐ PORTA-POTTY ☐ VACANT LOT

CHILDREN

☐ SKYSCRAPER ☐ MANSION ☐ FIXER-UPPER ☐ TRAILER HOME ☐ PORTA-POTTY ☐ VACANT LOT

PERSONAL DEVELOPMENT

☐ SKYSCRAPER ☐ MANSION ☐ FIXER-UPPER ☐ TRAILER HOME ☐ PORTA-POTTY ☐ VACANT LOT

HOPES, DREAMS, VISIONS FOR YOUR FUTURE

☐ SKYSCRAPER ☐ MANSION ☐ FIXER-UPPER ☐ TRAILER HOME ☐ PORTA-POTTY ☐ VACANT LOT

> **THE TRUTH IS, YOU CAN'T BUILD A SKYSCRAPER-SIZED VISION ON FIXER-UPPER FAITH, AND YOU WON'T EXPERIENCE MANSION-SIZED MIRACLES WITH PORTA-POTTY PRINCIPLES.**

fixer-upper faith, and you won't experience mansion-sized miracles with porta-potty principles. But let's take it a step further. Think about some specific areas of your life, and then rate your faith foundation for each one. Your friendships, career goals, romantic relationship, health (mental, emotional, spiritual, or physical), finances, children, business, personal development, and any other hopes, dreams, or visions for your future—each and every one needs to be built on a deep, sturdy faith foundation. Be honest, though: What kind of foundation are they on *right now*? Take a minute to plot it out.

No matter where you land, the exciting news is, this is just the beginning of our 𝕮𝖗𝖆𝖟𝖞 𝕱𝖆𝖎𝖙𝖍 journey. Whether your foundation is at vacant-lot status or has skyscraper capacity, your faith still has room to grow. We can all aspire to a deeper foundational level of faith.

Remember, 𝕮𝖗𝖆𝖟𝖞 𝕱𝖆𝖎𝖙𝖍 is about progression, not perfection.

WHAT IS CRAZY FAITH?

A simple definition of *faith* is "trust in something you cannot explicitly prove." Today, people google everything and tend to believe only things they can prove without a doubt. This makes having faith a challenge, so actually witnessing people act on faith is increasingly rare. Too often, *the facts that we see erode the faith that we need.* I'm sure you'd agree that this world we live in is pretty out of whack, and for things to get right, we need miracles taking place far more often. If we really want crazy results, we've got to put in a crazy amount of faith—even if it's hard. So I've got one question for you: *How badly do you want it?*

Merriam-Webster defines *crazy* as "not mentally sound: marked by thought or action that lacks reason." In other words, if something is crazy, it makes zero sense. There's no reasonable explanation why it should be happening. Some synonyms for *crazy* are *insane, impractical, erratic, out of the ordinary,* and *unusual.* You can probably think of someone you know who fits that description—and if you can't . . . well, then, it might be you!

I'm kidding. But for real, how many times have you called something crazy because it seemed impractical or unusual or out of your comfort zone? Can you think of someone who has become famous, popular, or respected for doing something the world considered crazy?

You're going to want to highlight this: I define 𝕮𝖗𝖆𝖟𝖞 𝕱𝖆𝖎𝖙𝖍 as "having thoughts and actions that lack reason but trusting fully in what you cannot explicitly prove." It reminds me of this old song that was made popular in 2006 by Gnarls Barkley—singer CeeLo Green and his producer, Danger Mouse—called "Crazy." The part that caught my attention at first was the chorus, but when I

> **TOO OFTEN, THE FACTS THAT WE SEE ERODE THE FAITH THAT WE NEED.**

> I DEFINE CRAZY FAITH AS "HAVING THOUGHTS AND ACTIONS THAT LACK REASON BUT TRUSTING FULLY IN WHAT YOU CANNOT EXPLICITLY PROVE."

looked up the lyrics, something about the last verse stuck with me. It says, "My heroes had the heart to lose their lives out on the limb, and all I remember is thinkin' I wanna be like them." That line always gets me thinking about the heroes we talk about every Sunday in church. The reason we're still talking about them to this day is that somewhere along their journeys, they had faith to live (and sometimes lose!) their lives out on the limb. Even in the face of people who called them crazy, many of these biblical heroes believed so deeply in what God had called them to do that they became martyrs for the cause of Christ.

I can't help but think about my own life as a believer and wonder if people will remember me as a guy who was crazy enough to live his life in faith out on the limb. Will my actions cause somebody to say, "I want to have the faith of Michael Todd"? It's great that we talk about Abraham and Ruth and David, but will people ever say anything about me or you? Will your coworkers be able to say, "My friend was truly a person of faith"? Will your kids and grandkids know you as someone who wasn't afraid to step out and act on your faith in God?

Think about someone you look up to or esteem highly. You celebrate that person because she dared to travel a road that most others haven't. The sad truth about **Crazy Faith** is that most believers *don't* live their lives out on the limb. They live safe, quiet lives and never get to see the full promise of God.

This may not sound like the most theologically proper way of presenting a biblical truth, but some things God asks His people to do seem absolutely crazy. Sometimes He'll ask you to do things that don't seem rational or logical at all, things people misunderstand or even make fun of. The Bible is full of stories just like that.

Take my boy Noah for example. He spent a ridiculous amount of time cutting down trees and building an enormous boat that sat on dry land in the middle of town where everybody could see and clown him publicly. You see, he'd heard from the Lord that a flood was coming, but up until that time nobody had ever seen rain. Everybody thought Noah had no sense—that is, until it started raining. Call me crazy, but I believe the soundtrack blasting from the boat's speakers at that moment was a paraphrased version of Mike Jones's hit song, "Back then, you didn't want me. Now I'm hot, you all on me." Noah was like, "Told you so! You're not getting on this boat, baby. Sorry, not sorry. You should have believed the word of the Lord!"

Okay, okay. Maybe it didn't happen *exactly* like that, but you get my drift, right? Everybody thought Noah's actions were crazy. If you were there, you might have thought so too.

But let Noah's story challenge you.

Maybe the thing you wrote down in your journal seems crazy now, but it's only crazy until it starts raining.

Maybe you're faithfully working a job you don't really like so that you can remain financially stable until the side-hustle, entrepreneurial venture you've been passionately pursuing takes off. Maybe people around you are telling you to give it up and settle for a nine-to-five, but something inside you can't let go of what you believe God told you would happen.

Maybe it seems crazy to save yourself in purity right now because the world tells you to just go out and do whatever you want with whomever you want.

> WHAT SEEMS CRAZY IN ONE SEASON WILL BE COUNTED AS FAITH IN ANOTHER.

Maybe it seems crazy to wake up at the crack of dawn, go into your daughter's bedroom, and write down a vision statement that declares you will own a 163,000-square-foot arena that will one day become the headquarters of your worldwide ministry. (True story. More on it later.)

But maybe—*just maybe*—what seems crazy in one season will be counted as faith in another.

It's only crazy until it happens, and maybe the fact that you stick to your guns and stand firm in your faith will be the deciding factor in someone else's heart and help him turn his eyes toward Jesus!

God wants you to be His modern-day hero. He wants people to be able to look at the faith *you* have and model their own after it. The faith you have to start the business in the middle of an economic crisis, to believe for a healing that doctors deem impossible, to let go and move forward after a devastating heartbreak—*your* 𝕮𝖗𝖆𝖟𝖞 𝕱𝖆𝖎𝖙𝖍 is what He wants to use to make a miracle happen. He's not looking for somebody to give Him all the reasons why it can't happen. He's looking for somebody to believe that if He says it, it *will* happen.

TRUE STORIES OF CRAZY FAITH

I've personally seen quite a few stories of 𝕮𝖗𝖆𝖟𝖞 𝕱𝖆𝖎𝖙𝖍 play out in my lifetime. The stories you are about to read are 100 percent true and have become amazing examples for me and many others to follow. It's time for us to start taking cues from heroes of the Christian faith who have gone before us, and I'm not just talking about people in the Bible. I'm talking about learning from heroes that are right in front of us, like Transformation Church's founding pastors, Bishop Gary and Pastor Debbie McIntosh, who had the faith to do something crazy. Let me paint the picture for you.

The north side of Tulsa, Oklahoma, where Gary and Debbie planted a church, has historically been inhabited mostly by African American families. In 1921, a devastating race massacre took place in a prominent upper-class district of North Tulsa called Greenwood, where many distinguished Black people lived and owned thriving businesses.* The area was known as Black Wall Street because it was a uniquely affluent national epicenter of economic prosperity for African Americans. Close to one-tenth of the population of the city of Tulsa back then was Black, and most of them lived in the Black Wall Street area.† Some white people saw this prosperous, expanding district as a threat to their comfortably segregated lives and allowed their hearts to be filled with hatred, like a pot of boiling water on a hot stove.

* "Tulsa Race Massacre," History.com, May 26, 2021, www.history.com /topics/roaring-twenties/tulsa-race-massacre.

† Alexis Clark, "Tulsa's 'Black Wall Street' Flourished as a Self-Contained Hub in Early 1900s," History.com, January 27, 2021, www.history.com /news/black-wall-street-tulsa-race-massacre.

On May 30, 1921, racial tensions came to an explosive head. A young Black teenager stepped onto the elevator of a fancy office building, and moments later, the young white elevator operator screamed of foul play. After the teen's arrest the next morning, angry white mobs assembled in the streets and by evening were burning Black businesses and homes to the ground without remorse. Hundreds of innocent people were murdered in violent attacks. Those eighteen-plus hours of chaos caused immense devastation that Black people are still working to recover from a century later. An already-divided city was torn apart.*

Many years later, in 1999, a man and woman of God heard the Spirit of the Lord calling them to start a ministry in that very part of Tulsa. Now, if you have never seen the McIntoshes, I want to give you some information to help you understand the context. They are white. Like, *white* white. Like Snow White white, with a side of Barry-Manilow-mixed-with-Neil-Diamond white. Nevertheless, they were convinced that God was calling them to the Blackest part of the city, and they acted on their 𝕮𝖗𝖆𝖟𝖞 𝕱𝖆𝖎𝖙𝖍. They moved across town. They rented out a space. Pastor Debbie started hosting small-group prayer meetings with some friends. And then one day, Bishop Gary drove downtown to the corner of Greenwood and Archer—the exact location where the devastating fires of the race massacre were sparked seventy-eight years earlier—and he heard the Spirit say, *Take off your shoes.*

Take off my shoes? Outside? He looked around and thought, *This is crazy. What if somebody sees me?* But still he obeyed. He took off his shoes right then and there—and right

* "Tulsa Race Massacre."

then and there, God said to him, *I want you to reverse the curse in North Tulsa.* Can you even imagine?

Gary and Debbie started a church not where it was easy but where they were called. They were obedient and stepped out in faith—and over the course of twenty years, a group of forty dedicated people meeting weekly in a downtown strip mall has become more than four thousand people gathering in an arena to experience a ministry that helps transform the lives of people of all races worldwide. It gives me enormous joy to honor them any chance I get, because Transformation Church wouldn't be what it is today if not for the 𝕮𝖗𝖆𝖟𝖞 𝕱𝖆𝖎𝖙𝖍 of Bishop Gary and Pastor Debbie McIntosh.

I wouldn't be writing this book and pursuing the purpose of God without the 𝕮𝖗𝖆𝖟𝖞 𝕱𝖆𝖎𝖙𝖍 of my parents, Brenda and Tommy Todd. Over thirty years ago, when they lived in New Orleans, Louisiana, they heard from a man of God who was starting a church in Tulsa. He told them, "You should come visit Tulsa." What they heard was "You should *move* to Tulsa." Now I don't know whose version of the story is right, but in the end, it was definitely God's will for them to be here. They left the comfort of what they knew and moved to a town where they knew only one other person. They began a journey of faith that would produce so much life and freedom in others—praying dozens of ministries forward and serving with everything they had—all while trusting God in 𝕮𝖗𝖆𝖟𝖞 𝕱𝖆𝖎𝖙𝖍.

My dad initially worked for the State Farm insurance company, but he and my mom sought God and decided that they were going to stop trusting in that system for finances because they felt God calling them into full-time ministry. This was crazy! They had children. They had a mortgage. They had bills. But crazy or not, my dad said, "This will be my last year working at State Farm, and we're going to believe God for everything that comes into this house."

(Now, I bet some of you reading this are thinking, *Oh, I'm quitting my job tomorrow!* But let me caution you: you'd better be sure you heard it from God, or you're going to be on an involuntary fast for a long time!)

Over and over again, I experienced God supernaturally provide for the Todd family, who had five hungry boys to feed and no groceries in the refrigerator. My mom would get down on her knees and pray, and the next morning the doorbell would ring and there would be nobody there—just a week's worth of groceries on the front porch. Nobody can convince me that believing God does not work!

HE NEEDS WILLING VESSELS.

Through the years, I have witnessed my parents sacrifice and give and trust God and give some more. Then I've watched God not only meet our needs but also bless us with more than enough to share with others. Their ministry has gone on to impact millions of people around the globe, all because they keep saying yes to God.

I hope you feel inspired when you read the stories I tell in this book—but more than that, I hope you are compelled. I hope you glimpse how many other stories are waiting to be told. There are destinies waiting to be altered, hearts waiting to be turned, lives waiting to be transformed, inventions waiting to be created, buildings waiting to be designed, philosophies waiting to be shaped, and a world desperately waiting for answers that can come only from the God who created it.

But He needs something too. He needs willing vessels. God's Word says that all creation is groaning, waiting for the sons and daughters of God to be revealed (Romans 8:18–23). God is ready to load and fire some spiritual weapons of mass destruction aimed at the devil's territory, but He needs some all-in believers who will trust Him and step out in 𝕮𝖗𝖆𝖟𝖞 𝕱𝖆𝖎𝖙𝖍.

You ready?

2

BABY FAITH

YOU'VE GOT TO CRAWL BEFORE YOU WALK

I know some of you are looking at the title of this chapter and saying, "Now, Mike, didn't you just tell me to have 𝕮𝖗𝖆𝖟𝖞 𝕱𝖆𝖎𝖙𝖍? Isn't that the name of this book?" Yes, absolutely, and we'll get to that. But first, we've got to start somewhere. No one walks into a gym for the first time in two years and jumps into bench-pressing three hundred pounds, and nobody in her right mind jumps headfirst into a pool for the first time and expects to perform like an Olympic swimmer.

The night I first met Natalie, I didn't get down on one knee, profess my undying love, and propose to her. She would have called me desperate! Instead, I took my time to get to know her, cracked a few jokes, spit some game, got the digits . . . you know, baby steps. Look, baby steps are annoying, but they are absolutely necessary to reach a big goal. Lifting heavier weights calls for gradual conditioning, and managing greater success calls for steady character building. You've got to do your reps.

But don't get it twisted: it takes great faith to take baby steps too.

𝕮𝖗𝖆𝖟𝖞 𝕱𝖆𝖎𝖙𝖍 is not where you start; it is where you find yourself after you're diligent and dedicated to exercising baby faith. But the truth is, most people who want to be great don't want to do anything on a small scale. They want Moses-parting-the-Red-Sea types of results, but they don't want to go back to Egypt and face their pasts. They want to be safe on a giant, sturdy boat in the middle of a flood, but they don't want splinters from sanding down the wooden planks needed to build it. I imagine that for Noah, cutting down that first tree took a small measure of faith and a huge amount of humility that nobody saw except him and God.

> CRAZY FAITH IS NOT WHERE YOU START; IT IS WHERE YOU FIND YOURSELF AFTER YOU'RE DILIGENT AND DEDICATED TO EXERCISING BABY FAITH.

For you, baby faith might mean opening a bank account that you label Generosity Fund and depositing five dollars in it. Baby faith might look like filling out an application to enroll in an evening class at your local junior college. It might mean browsing your local furniture store and picking out the new sectional that you want to put in the living room of the new house you don't yet own. Baby faith might mean writing a letter to that parent you haven't spoken to in years.

I believe that soon you'll be sprinting forward in your faith, but you can't run if you don't learn to walk first. You may have never heard it said like this before, but walking in faith comes from crawling in faith. And it's okay to crawl. (Cue "Crawl" by Chris Brown.)

> WALKING IN FAITH COMES FROM CRAWLING IN FAITH. AND IT'S OKAY TO CRAWL.

IMAGINE THAT

If you can't figure out what your first step of faith should be, God has given you an amazing tool to walk in baby faith. It's called your imagination. That's right, your imagination. Now, I need you to do something that might seem a little crazy, depending on where you're reading this book. (If you're on the treadmill, proceed with caution.) Close your eyes. No, seriously; read the next few sentences, and then close your eyes.

Imagine yourself in your favorite vacation spot, sitting next to someone who makes you happy and sipping unlimited refills of your favorite drink. You've got ten seconds. *Go!*

Ahh . . . didn't that feel good? It's okay if you took longer than ten seconds. I want you to understand the power of your imagination. I'm sitting in my office writing these words to you, but in my mind, I just went to Aruba. I could smell salt water. I could feel warm white sand between my toes, hear the laughter of children playing nearby, and see Natalie lounging on the beach chair next to me. I could taste the cool, refreshing virgin piña colada, with three cherries and a shot of grenadine, that I could see myself drinking from a pineapple in my hand.

Excuse me while I book a flight right now.

Imagination is not mere child's play; it is a powerful force given to us by our Creator. Its root word is *image,* and we are created in the image of God with the power to imagine what is not yet tangible but can be realized. That's crazy! You may have stopped using your imagination because somebody said you need to grow up and start adulting, but I'm telling you, it's time to revive it again. Imagination is way too powerful to be left sitting in the toy box.

You can be sitting in a place that is the exact opposite of what you desire, then close your eyes and see yourself exactly where you want to be. (Go ahead; do it again!) You could be bedridden in a full body cast, but when you close your eyes, you can imagine

> **WE ARE CREATED IN THE IMAGE OF GOD WITH THE POWER TO IMAGINE WHAT IS NOT YET TANGIBLE BUT CAN BE REALIZED.**

yourself healed and walking again. You and your kids could wake up in your one-bedroom apartment listening to water drip into a bucket under the most recent ceiling leak, but then you close your eyes and see yourself being handed the keys to your beautiful new four-bedroom, two-bath home in a safe, quiet neighborhood. You could be at Christmas dinner sitting next to your drunk uncle John with other family members arguing across the table but then close your eyes and see a peaceful, joyful family get-together where everyone is showing each other love and sharing testimonies of God's faithfulness. You could even be in a jail cell, counting down the days until you're able to hold your child again, but when you close your eyes, through the power of imagination, you're at her seventh birthday party, snapping pics with glittery unicorns and princess tiaras.

Don't belittle your imagination! It's God given. It's divine. Those daydreams could be God trying to show you a glimpse of the future that is possible for you if you would only believe Him enough to move toward it. No matter how small your baby step is, taking it still requires faith. And trust me, there is *big* power in small faith. I'll show you.

FAITH IN SEED FORM

In Matthew 17, there's a story about a time when Jesus's disciples are on crowd-control duty (verse 14). Everything is going fine until this one father asks them to pray for his demon-possessed son. Jesus had given the disciples authority to heal sick people and cast out demons (10:1), so why not? They muster up the courage to lay hands on this boy, and . . . pause for effect . . . *nothing happens.*

The boy's father does what my dad would do if we were at a restaurant and the server didn't bring us what we asked for: he asks to speak to their boss. He approaches Jesus, Jesus rebukes the demon, and instantly the boy is healed! That makes the disciples wonder why it didn't work when they tried.

This reminds me of a time a while back when my oldest daughter, Isabella, was trying hard to beat a level on her favorite game on my phone. Seeing her on the brink of giving up in frustration, I asked her to let me try. Not only did I beat the level, but I also got the new high score. I winked at her and explained that I had faced that villain before and already knew all his tricks. Isabella may still have been intimidated by the villain, but I had the confidence to beat him—and she begged me to teach her to do it herself.

Jesus is never scared of opposition, especially the kind the disciples are facing, and He has the greatest response when they ask Him why they hadn't been able to beat the villain: "You don't have enough faith. . . . I tell you the truth, if you had faith even as small as a mustard seed . . . nothing would be impossible" (17:20). Let me remix it for you: Jesus tells them if they'd had only baby faith for the boy's healing, he would have been healed.

That challenges me to think how much authority God has given us. Think about how much power is packed into something as petite as baby faith!

I imagine Jesus looking around for the biggest example He can find, seeing the silhouette of a mountain in the distance, and adding, "You could say to this mountain, 'Move from here to there,' and it would move" (verse 20). I don't know if you've ever seen a real mountain up close, but they're pretty gigantic. And in case you've never seen a real mustard seed, well, here you go:

That's how much faith Jesus said it would take for you to move a mountain, to dissolve $150,000 worth of debt, to heal a person dying of cancer, to go from being homeless to owning a neighborhood full of houses. Not mountain-sized faith but mustard-seed faith (a.k.a. *baby faith*). Nothing about a mustard seed seems powerful. I bet if I threw a mustard seed at you as hard as I could, you wouldn't even notice.

But let me encourage you: God sees it, heaven notices, and the entire supernatural realm feels it when we step out in baby faith! You might not be able to see the mountain moving right away, but you have no idea what's going on under the surface, how God is working on your behalf behind the scenes as you do your reps to condition your faith muscles.

Sadly, though, many of us don't even try because from

> OUR FAITH IS NOT IN OURSELVES AND OUR OWN ABILITIES BUT IN THE OMNIPOTENT GOD IN WHOM WE TRUST.

our perspective everything looks like an immovable mountain. Perhaps our culture is so built around microwavable, instant, two-day-shipping convenience that we have trouble grasping the worth and value of a baby step. After all, if I set a huge goal and take only tiny steps toward it every so often, I might eventually get there but it will take an exhausting amount of time, endurance, and patience.

The difference for believers is that our faith is not in ourselves and our own abilities but in the omnipotent God in whom we trust.

My friend works for a company that offers her great benefits, including a 401(k) retirement plan with dollar-for-dollar matching. So, for every dollar she puts into the account, her employer contributes another dollar. Many would say this is a great benefit, but it doesn't even compare to the blessings God has for believers who trust Him. For every small thing you do in baby faith, God meets you with multiplied results. Through the power and grace of Christ Jesus, the potency of your small amount of faith is exponentially increased—and the best part is, *you* get to experience the return on *His* investment.

CHILDLIKE TRUST

At the beginning of Matthew 18, the disciples come to Jesus and ask, "Who is greatest in the Kingdom of Heaven?" (verse

1). If I were Jesus, I would have replied, "Are you serious? Why do you even need to know that?" Aren't you glad Jesus is always so patient with us when we're insecure and trying to compete with each other instead of simply having faith that God has a great plan for each one of us?

Jesus begins His response to His disciples' question by pointing to a little child—not an astute, wise, experienced, or prolific adult but a baby. "I tell you the truth," He says, "unless you turn from your sins and become like little children, you will never get into the Kingdom of Heaven" (verse 3). He continues with His teaching moment: the only way to become the greatest in the kingdom is to become as humble as a little kid (verse 4). He is trying to get these grown-up, religious men with little faith to understand this about children: *they trust first*. They are born with baby faith and act on it regularly. They believe what adults tell them because they have no past experiences that fuel their fears. There are no conditions on their trust.

This is how God wants us to trust in Him and His plans for us.

When my children are hungry, they don't ask how much money is in the bank account or whether we have time to feed them. They trust that, as parental providers, Natalie and I have already prepared something for them to eat. They don't fear that they won't have a place to sleep tonight. They trust their parents to take care of that. I have resolved to be a loving, active father, so I make sure my children are taken care of. If they need or want anything, they are not afraid to ask me for it.

I've been blessed with an amazing earthly father who isn't perfect but does his best through Christ to show me what the love of our heavenly Father looks like when it's manifested on earth. It's pretty easy to trust my dad because when he says something, I can take it to the bank.

Do you have that kind of faith in your heavenly Father?

Take a moment to think about yourself as a child, and let me ask you a personal question: Did you trust your earthly father? What you experienced was unique to you and has shaped you in many ways, but maybe you haven't realized how your relationship with your earthly father directly affects how you view or experience your heavenly Father today.

I recognize not everyone has a dependable dad. Perhaps your story is similar to my friend Jenna's. Her dad passed away when she was eleven years old, just as she was about to enter the adolescent years that would shape the woman she'd eventually become. Jenna spent years trying to fill the void of losing her father by putting her trust in men who were more like selfish, immature boys who took advantage of her over and over again. This pattern continued into adulthood, where she endured broken and abusive situationships that left her feeling as unprotected and alone as that eleven-year-old girl. She had a hard time developing committed relationships with anyone, secretly fearing that each person might leave her the way her dad had. She knew it wasn't his fault that he was gone, but she still partially blamed him for not being there for her.

Maybe you identify more with my bro Nick, who was almost an adult the first time he met his biological father. Growing up, he couldn't help but notice how many of his friends had both of their parents around for special occasions. His mom never talked much about his father, except to say that she and Nick were better off without him. Even so, Nick asked about him all the time. Finally, on Nick's sixteenth birthday, his dad called the house. It turned out he had been living just outside town for ten years but had never made the effort to visit his son. To top it all off, he was married and had a daughter—meaning, Nick had a sister. Nick was crushed to find this out but also felt hopeful that he could develop a relationship with his father. He invited him to award ceremonies, birthday parties, and holiday get-togethers, and his father always promised he was coming. But the only thing Nick could trust about him was that he would let him down by not showing up.

If you had an absent father or a parent who fell significantly short of giving you the love, care, provision, and attention that you craved as a child, it may be hard to have childlike faith in a Father you cannot physically see. Psychological studies tell us that we human beings tend to associate the attributes of our primary father figure (or lack thereof) with God.* If you couldn't count on your earthly father, it's harder, statistically speaking, for you to put your trust in God. You may have a tendency to correlate the earthly dad who never showed up for your birthday parties and soccer games with a heavenly Father who won't come through when you need Him.

Yet this couldn't be further from the truth. God is actually omnipresent, which means present *always and everywhere;* it's just that He's invisible. And it's more difficult for someone who already has a hard heart to have faith in something or someone he can't physically see. One of the names of Jesus is Immanuel, which means "God is with us" (Matthew 1:23). The real question is, Are we aware of His presence?

---

* John Bishop, *God Distorted: How Your Earthly Father Affects Your Perception of God and Why It Matters* (Colorado Springs: Multnomah, 2013), chap. 1.

> ## DON'T ALLOW UNFORGIVENESS TO HARDEN YOUR HEART TO THE ONLY LOVE THAT CAN HEAL YOU.

What I'm asking you to do in this moment is to allow the Holy Spirit to soften your heart so you can forgive your earthly father and let God be Abba, Daddy, your Father in heaven who will never die, never disappoint you, never leave you, and never reject you. God is the Father who has been with you all along. Don't allow unforgiveness to harden your heart to the only love that can heal you.

We may not be able to see God Himself in the flesh, but we can see His provision, feel His love for us, and live surrounded by the grace and favor He gives His children. God is a loving, active Father. He's never made a promise that He didn't keep, and His Word is *full* of great and precious promises. He wants to help you learn to trust again and to lean on Him like a little child should be able to lean on her dad. He knows that you may not be ready to run full speed into His arms yet, and He's okay with that. He just wants you to take a few baby steps in faith. You can start by simply acknowledging Him. All it takes for Him to turn around an impossible situation is a mustard seed of baby faith.

RUDIMENTARY FAITH

My daughter Ava Rae started walking at eleven months. A few weeks prior to that, her chunky thighs had built up enough muscle from crawling and bouncing in her walker, but her mind had not yet built up enough confidence to carry her. But one day she decided enough was enough. She was determined to reach her sippy cup on the coffee table across the room, and even though both her parents were there, she wanted to exercise her independence. (Did I mention she is sassy?)

She stood up, took three wobbly steps, and then . . . *smack!* She fell on her bottom. She looked up at us, and her lower lip quivered, but we applauded and cheered and encouraged her to do it again. (Side note: Get yourself a community who will cheer for you and encourage you in your baby steps! We'll talk more about this later.)

With a bit of hesitation—because she didn't want to fall again—Ava turned over and put her little feet back on the ground. By this time, her big brother and sister had wandered into the living room and joined in on the encouragement, smiling and clapping, excited and anticipating her next steps. She made it to her feet and tried again. It took a few more tries after that, but guess what, y'all: Ava Rae reached her sippy cup!

She didn't get up and start running. She took baby steps. Running came later and only because she did what she was capable of at the time. At eleven months, each and every step she took was momentous. Each step was a miracle. Each step was a memory. Each step brought momentum. Each step was movement forward.

I want to encourage your faith the same way I encouraged my daughter. Each and every step you

> **EACH AND EVERY STEP YOU TAKE IN BABY FAITH IS A MOMENTOUS OCCASION THAT'S BRINGING MOMENTUM FOR YOUR MIRACLE.**

take in baby faith is a momentous occasion that's bringing momentum for your miracle. People may not understand how valuable your pint-sized progression toward purpose really is, but don't let anybody make you feel bad for working your muscle of faith. Every step out of your comfort zone is momentous. Each step past fear makes you a walking miracle. Every time you share your testimony is monumental. The words you speak in faith bring momentum. Even your attempt to grow your faith by reading this book is movement forward.

Do not despise these small beginnings, for the LORD rejoices to see the work begin. (Zechariah 4:10)

For some of you, taking steps of baby faith means going back to the basics. Maybe it's not your first time stepping out, but it can still be hard to start over and start small.

I started playing drums when I was literally a baby, about two years old, and my first "drum set" was a random assortment of my mom's pots, pans, and Tupperware. Over time, my parents saw my love for percussion and noticed I had a natural gift, so they invested in it and bought me a junior pro drum set . . . which I busted a hole through on the first day. Next came the upgraded set—it had shiny gold cymbals and a real kick pedal!—but it lasted only a month. Then, for my eighth birthday, my wonderful parents gave me a professional Tama Rockstar double-bass kit that my dad won at auction as a State Farm agent. I looked like a little gnome sitting behind that big drum set, but I was in second-grader heaven!

Whether it was the table in the lunchroom, the bleachers in the gym, or the dashboard of my dad's Jeep, I always found something to tap or bang on, relentless in my desire to sharpen my talent. I drove my brothers crazy with late-night practice, trying to perfect the latest drum pattern I'd heard on the radio—but I knew it would pay off in the long run.

When I was in middle school, my parents started me in drum lessons. At the time, I was consistently playing semiprofessionally for my church and for my mom when she traveled across the country to various churches. I was good for my age—actually, I was *really* good for my age, but my dad knew there was so much more in me.

I will never forget my first lesson. I was hyped! I came in ready to impress my instructor with all the tricks I had taught myself. But he had a different plan. After I finished what I believed to be the greatest drum solo in the history of all humankind, my instructor kindly invited me to step away from the drum set . . . and handed me a pillow. I was confused. *Does he think I deserve a nap after exerting all that energy?* Nope. He explained that for at least the next year, I would not be practicing on an actual drum set. My assignment was to practice *rudiments,* to bang basic beats on a pillow.

To say I was shocked is an understatement. All I could think was, *This is kid stuff. How is this going to make me better?*

Now for anyone who's not familiar with rudiments, let me break them down for you. Drum rudiments are very basic rhythmic patterns found in common musical styles that are used as repetitive exercises for performers to hone their technical skills. Rudiments are to a drummer what scales are to a singer, what free throws are to a basketball player, what chopping vegetables is to a chef: *boooooorrrrriiiing!*

Before I started drum lessons, my pride had built me up to believe I was already playing at a professional level. And the truth is, I *was* talented. But I lacked the discipline, precision, and consistency that can come only with practicing rudiments. I had a whole Karate Kid versus Mr. Miyagi wake-up call: wax on, wax off. Right, left, right, right, left, right, left, left (that's a paradiddle for anyone who wants to know). I had to go back to the basics and learn to be satisfied with the small and seemingly insignificant.

Remember in the last chapter when we talked about faith foundations? Practicing rudiments was the equivalent of lifting up a house with cracked walls and misaligned doors to rebuild its foundation. After I dedicated that season to learning the basics, my drum-playing capabilities went to a whole new level of accuracy, speed, and complexity, a level I *never* would have reached if I hadn't submitted to what seemed small. It also revolutionized the way I hear music and rhythm, making me a much better music producer. Even more, it planted in me a deep conviction about the absolute necessity of baby steps.

The same way God multiplied my gift back to me is the way that He desires to multiply your faith back to you. You may not be able to see the whole path now, but if you're willing to take a small step and commit to consistently walking in baby faith, He's ready to reveal more of it to you.

IT'S NOT TOO SMALL

For a long time in my Christian life, I was convinced that certain things were below God's care-o-meter. There were small things I chose not to bother God with because I assumed He had bigger things to be concerned about. What I didn't realize was that those small situations were opportunities to rely on Him. Proverbs 3:6 says, "In all your ways acknowledge Him, and He shall direct your paths" (NKJV). Many people tend to exclude or deemphasize the word *all* in that verse. But *all* encompasses small things too. The inconsequential, minor, measly, not-that-big-of-a-deal, tiny, trivial details of our lives—*all* of them matter to God. Remember, the baby faith you exercise in one season will build your faith muscle to believe Him for the big things coming later.

What seems too small for others to care about is just the right size for God. You may think, *God doesn't care if I get a good parking spot at the mall* or *God doesn't care about this car payment* or *God doesn't care whether my hair grows back*. But the truth is, God cares about what we care about, no matter how small, simply because we are His children. If it hurts us, He feels it. If it's important to us, it's important to our Father. When we exclude God from any part of our lives, it shows Him where our faith really lies. I would never want my kids to think I don't care about their scraped knees or the toys they want for Christmas. I want them to feel completely confident that they can come to me about anything. The answer may not always be yes, but I will always do what I believe is best to help them heal and grow and be examples to others.

Since the days of Adam and Eve, God has always desired for His children to trust Him enough to run to Him. First Peter 5:7 tells us to give *all* our worries and cares to God because He cares about us. In Matthew 21:22 Jesus says, "You can pray for anything, and if you have faith, you will receive it."

Do you really believe that? Too

> WHAT SEEMS TOO SMALL FOR OTHERS TO CARE ABOUT IS JUST THE RIGHT SIZE FOR GOD.

many people don't, and they are living beneath their means as a child of the King.

We can pray and ask God about *anything*—school tuition, parenting, love, peace, joy, money, family, friends, favor, our future, our fears, hard conversations, dreams, a new computer, wisdom, relationships, the best route home from work, the best Chinese food in the city we're visiting (I pray about this one a lot).

Anything.

Prayer should be our first response, not our last resort. Too often, however, people turn to God only when they're at the end of their ropes or when something earth-shattering happens. This was my routine for years, praying only when I was in trouble or on trial. Can you identify? In the weeks following the 9/11 terrorist attacks, church attendance in the US surged as much as 24 percent.* Online attendance at church services and Google searches for faith-based subjects skyrocketed after the whole world shut down in 2020 due to a global pandemic.† Don't get me wrong: in those times, it was necessary to pray. But I would much rather we intercede when something is in infancy than wait until it becomes enormous.

> **PRAYER SHOULD BE OUR FIRST RESPONSE, NOT OUR LAST RESORT.**

---

* Andrew Walsh, "Returning to Normalcy," *Religion in the News* 5, no. 1 (Spring 2002), www2.trincoll.edu/csrpl/RINVol5No1/returning%20 normalcy.htm.

† David Roach, "Coronavirus Searches Lead Millions to Hear About Jesus," *Christianity Today*, April 7, 2020, www.christianitytoday.com/news /2020/april/coronavirus-searches-online-converts-pray-cru-bgea-wmo.html.

Practically speaking, there's nothing wrong with NyQuil or Tylenol, but when was the last time you acknowledged God first and prayed about your headache instead of reaching into the medicine cabinet? Everyone wants to get together and pray when John has a heart attack and is having emergency surgery. And again, that is *definitely* the right time to pray. But it's also the right time to acknowledge God and pray when you're hiring a new receptionist for your office. It's also the right time to acknowledge God and pray when you and your wife have an argument on the way home from the store. It's also the right time to acknowledge God and pray when you're doing your makeup in the morning and you wish your eyebrows would grow so you wouldn't have to fill them in so much. It's also the right time to acknowledge God and pray whenever you think about praying! What I'm trying to say is, it's *always* the right time to pray. If it's important to you, it's important to God.

Jesus said it Himself. It's in red print and everything. *You can pray for anything.* If you want to have 𝕮𝖗𝖆𝖟𝖞 𝕱𝖆𝖎𝖙𝖍, it's time for you to stop discounting the things that call for baby faith. You're hoping for God to one day make you a philanthropist who pays off college tuitions and donates millions to charitable organizations, but you won't give God 10 percent of your retail-store paycheck right now. CEO status starts with the baby step of taking care of what you have now.

Yes, God *can* elevate you, expand your influence, and enlarge your impact, but He wants to see you trust Him right where you are first, *before* He takes you some-

> IT'S ALWAYS THE RIGHT TIME TO PRAY.

where else. That's called stewardship: simply recognizing that He's the true owner and originator of everything, while we're the ones who enjoy and take care of it all. Maybe it's His grace that is keeping you at level 1 until you learn the lessons necessary to help sustain you at level 10. There's nothing wrong with learning lessons at a low level. 𝕮𝖗𝖆𝖟𝖞 𝕱𝖆𝖎𝖙𝖍 develops as a result of consistently working your baby faith.

FUEL FOR YOUR FAITH

One of the Enemy's most effective tactics is to discourage you so much about your current circumstances that you don't hope anymore. Because if you lose hope, you will never have faith for anything. Hope is fuel for our faith. Remember, faith is the confidence in what we *hope* for.

Here's another opportunity for you to exercise your God-given imagination. Imagine someone handing you the keys to your favorite luxury vehicle—paid off, fully loaded, with customized interior and a brand-new paint job in the exact color you've always wanted. The only caveat is that the fuel tank is empty. Suddenly the trim package, sound system, and custom rims don't matter much if the vehicle doesn't have fuel to go anywhere. In the same way, if I don't have hope—fuel—I can't possibly move forward in this journey of faith.

> **HOPE IS FUEL FOR OUR FAITH.**

One of the saddest realities I encounter is when people are living life with no fuel, existing on empty, full of potential with plenty of horsepower but lacking hope's power to propel them toward a destination. Situation after situation, bill after bill, and bad relationship after bad relationship all try to convince them to give up hope. That's why we have to constantly remind ourselves where our hope is found. Hope is found in Jesus—in His words, His promises, His truth. He's the only one who was here before us, is here with us, and will never leave us. Hebrews 13:8 says, "Jesus Christ is the same yesterday, today, and forever." He is the source of our hope and He's forever trustworthy, so we can anchor our hope in Him.

The best thing about hope is that it's free. It doesn't cost a thing. You can do it right now. Faith, on the other hand, requires a little more sacrifice. It demands acts of obedience. It may instruct you to leave what's comfortable and convenient to pursue something that seems absolutely crazy; just look at the beginning of Abram's story in Genesis 12.

But hope is step one. You may have experienced so much disappointment that you have stopped hoping, but allow me to encourage you. Pick up your hope again. I dare you to hope that you'll become a homeowner, even though you're two months behind on your rent right now. Hope that God will turn your situation around and give you favor and provision. Hope that your wayward children who are rebelling against the rules you've set in your house will quit wildin' out, come to Christ, and live lifestyles that bring Him glory.

Every time you get a phone call from that one friend who's always into some type of drama, instead of saying, "Oh, God, here we go again," I challenge you to hope that maybe *this* is the moment God has brought him to the end of his rope and that he just needs a compassionate friend to pray with him.

Sure, you might be frustrated with your student loans. It's easy to assume you'll be making minimum payments until you die. But instead, I challenge you to hope that the entire balance will be forgiven or paid off.

Hope in spite of the negative report from your doctor.

Hope in spite of the balance in your bank account.

Hope in spite of the odds stacked against you.

Hope even when you got hurt hoping last time.

Hope again.

Our words and prayers and confessions have power, and the only way to start sparking confident faith is to allow yourself to hope again. What do you need to be hoping for?

I hope _____

_____

_____

_____

_____

Faith works in reverse. Culture tells us that we should be confident only in what is proven, seen, or experienced firsthand. But the truth is, whatever you hope for is how far your confidence can expand. If you're hoping to be able to live from month to month, to pay your bills from paycheck to paycheck, then that's as far as your confidence will grow. If fear has caused you to stop hoping for a happy, healthy marriage and all you're hoping is that you don't get cheated on or don't get a divorce, then you're settling for an extremely low level of hope—and I recommend you (shameless plug) read my book *Relationship Goals*. I understand that things have happened in life to hijack your hope, but I don't believe your journey is over. You have somewhere important to go and people waiting on you at that destination. But to get there, you need the fuel of faith. You need hope.

The goal is to trust that God is for you being healed, delivered, prosperous, and thriving. If you don't believe it, you won't expect it. If you don't expect it, you won't hope for it. And, ultimately, if you don't hope for it, you will take the fuel out of faith—because, remember, faith is confidence in what we *hope* for.

> **WHATEVER YOU HOPE FOR IS HOW FAR YOUR CONFIDENCE CAN EXPAND.**

I want to point you to our unfailing God and encourage you to hope that nothing is impossible *for Him*. If you need a healing, start hoping for it. If you need an upgrade, start hoping for it. Even if you're in a situation that looks hopeless, hope that God can bring you out of it. If you don't feel confident enough to hope for change yet, then start with a wish or a dream and ask God to develop it into hope. Restoration of hope is the beginning of baby faith.

Many of us get discouraged when we hope for something great but it doesn't happen right away. (We'll talk about timing and patience in a later chapter.) When you get your hopes up but then experience disappointment, it can leave you feeling vulnerable and afraid to take another baby step forward. I can't promise you'll never be disappointed by circumstances and other people, but God and His Word remain constant, faithful, and trustworthy. You can put your hope in Him.

> **RESTORATION OF HOPE IS THE BEGINNING OF BABY FAITH.**

We have to start somewhere, and we often have to start small. Most people don't want to do anything on a small scale because they fear feeling insignificant. But let me encourage you! There's big power in small faith, and faith starts with hope. I want to help fuel your faith because I want to see you healed and whole and fully trusting in God. We can take this journey one baby step at a time.

If your hope has been hijacked, here's a baby-step prayer to get you started:

God, it's hard to hope right now because of everything I've experienced. But today, I'm asking You to help me hope again (or even for the first time). Your Word says that You are the source of hope (Romans 15:13), so I pray that You will fill me today with joy and peace. I want to wholeheartedly trust You. Through the power of the Holy Spirit, I will soon overflow with confident hope. Amen.

3

MAYBE FAITH

A USEFUL WORD

As the parents of four small children who are becoming increasingly confident asking for what they want, Natalie and I have found that one of most useful words in the English language is *maybe*. *Maybe* means "perhaps," "possibly," "we'll see," or "yes with a hint of uncertainty."

"Daddy, can we get a slushy?"

"Maybe."

"Daddy, can we go to the park?"

"Maybe."

"Daddy, can we go to Disney World?

"Maybe."

"Daddy, can we get a dog?"

"No."

(Until Natalie chimes in, "Maybe.")

Because they know their father's nature, my children look at "maybe" optimistically. When Daddy says "maybe," they get their hopes up. They see possibilities instead of problems.

I'm encouraging you to adopt this principle. When somebody says "maybe," your first instinct might be to think of all the reasons it can't happen. But what if from now on, every

> ## MAYBE DOES NOT HAVE TO KILL YOUR MOMENTUM. IT *MAY BE* THE START OF A MIRACLE.

time you hear "maybe," you think of all the reasons it *can*?

In my faith journey, the word *maybe* has become unexpectedly valuable. It allows me to look at things that seem impossible and think, *Maybe God wants this for me.*

"Perhaps I can walk in that level of leadership."

"It's possible that my relationship could be whole."

"We'll see what comes from this step of baby faith."

"Yeah, it could happen even though I'm uncertain how."

"Maybe!"

Maybe does not have to kill your momentum. It *may be* the start of a miracle.

FIFTY-ONE PERCENT FAITH

How do you know you are moving in enough faith? How can you be confident that God is real, that He heard your prayer and is moving on your behalf right now? How can you be content, knowing that your future is safe? How can you be sure the thing you are believing for will actually happen? Are you *positive* you heard from God?

As a minister I get these sorts of questions all the time. My honest answer may shock you, but I'm going to give it to you anyway. You ready? Brace yourself. *You can't be sure. It's almost always a maybe.*

I'm willing to bet there aren't a lot of pastors who would

tell you the simple truth in such a blunt way, but I want to keep it 100 percent with you. This walk with Jesus is not based on facts, because you can never have *all* the facts; it's based on faith. Even when you're not sure about what's coming, you can be assured that Jesus doesn't start anything He doesn't intend to finish. He is

> ## FAITH IN GOD BEGINS WHERE HUMAN UNDERSTANDING ENDS.

"Jesus, the author and finisher of our faith" (Hebrews 12:2, NKJV).

Faith in God begins where human understanding ends. In other words, faith starts where we stop. When we acknowledge that we don't know everything and that there are things at work in our lives and in the world around us way beyond our ability to comprehend, faith begins. God's lowest thoughts are still higher than our greatest plans, programs, and philosophies—and accepting that takes humility.

"My thoughts are nothing like your thoughts," says the LORD.
"And my ways are far beyond anything you could
        imagine.
For just as the heavens are higher than the earth,
    so my ways are higher than your ways
    and my thoughts higher than your thoughts."
        (Isaiah 55:8–9)

When you open your mind to the possibility of a miracle and think to yourself, *Maybe that could actually happen,*

> # YOU DON'T HAVE TO BE SURE AS LONG AS YOU TRUST THAT GOD IS.

that's real faith. The *maybe* doesn't cancel out the faith. When you feel a strong impression that you're supposed to sell your business and move overseas for missions but then someone you respect questions your decision and asks, "Are you sure this is God?" it's okay to be in the gray space (I like to call it grace space) of not being completely sure. You don't have to be sure as long as you trust that God is. Faith is being okay with not knowing, okay with the maybe.

Faith grows as we learn more about the God who knows everything. I'm going to reiterate this point over and over again: progression, not perfection. Faith grows wherever it's planted, which is why it's so important that your faith be deeply rooted in the Word of God. The answers to your questions are not found in what you are believing for; they're found in whom you are believing in.

The idea of being 100 percent sure is overrated. We live in a world where skeptical, distrustful people enter into agreements only reluctantly. People don't want to extend trust right away. We like to know everything in advance because it makes us feel more in control of a situation. That's why so many contracts are full of manipulative legal jargon for everything from cable companies to record labels, as well as prenuptial agreements in case the couple that was so in love on their wedding day decides to split up. But that's not how faith works. Faith starts only when we realize we *aren't* in control and we *don't* know and begin to trust the One who is and does. We have to be only sure enough and confident enough to believe enough for Him to move in our lives.

So how much is *enough*?

If I conduct a highly scientific poll by asking one hundred people if they would choose chocolate or vanilla ice cream and fifty-one people say they prefer chocolate, then chocolate is the preference of the majority. If the ballots for an election are tallied and 51 percent of voters cast their ballots for one candidate, then she is the winner.

What am I getting at? I'm saying that 51 percent is enough to win. You might not be 100 percent sure, but God can work with 51 percent. Faith at 51 percent says, "I can't see the whole pathway, but Lord, I trust You enough to start walking anyway."

First Corinthians 13:9, 12 poetically describes how we as humans don't know everything. "We know in part and we prophesy in part. . . . We see in a mirror, dimly, but then face to face" (NKJV). We have only part of the picture until God Himself reveals the whole thing to us. In the meantime, He often shows us either the directions without the destination or the destination without the directions. Either way, our position should be to trust Him.

Think about marriage for a minute. Natalie and I met when she was fourteen and I was fifteen (crazy!). Through bad adolescent communication, dumb mistakes, breakups, makeups, and most definitely Crazy Faith, we made it to the altar on June 19, 2010. We were both twenty-three. The night before our wedding, a friend asked if I was 100 percent sure that Nat

> FAITH AT 51 PERCENT SAYS, "I CAN'T SEE THE WHOLE PATHWAY, BUT LORD, I TRUST YOU ENOUGH TO START WALKING ANYWAY."

was the person I wanted to spend the rest of my life with. Chest puffed out and bank account dwindling (weddings ain't cheap), I told him yes.

But as I reflect on it now, I wasn't 100 percent sure. How could I have been? I had never been married before. I had no experience waking up to a spouse's funky morning breath, managing finances with another person (who has opinions and ideas of her own!), or figuring out how to raise children on the same team. After counseling, prophecy, hours of prayer, and my decision, I was actually about 51 percent sure. Not 78 percent. Not 62 percent. I was 51 percent sure this was the woman I wanted to spend my life with—and that was enough to make a 100 percent promise.

No one who has ever done anything great for God has been 100 percent sure the entire time. If that person said he was, he lied! Abraham heard from the Lord that he should sacrifice his son Isaac, and he wasn't sure how that would pan out (Genesis 22). There was no way for him to know that God would provide a ram for the sacrifice and spare Isaac's life at the last second. He had to exercise faith at 51 percent. All he had to go on was a word from God, but that was enough to tip the scale and push his faith over the line.

When Joshua led the Israelites in a 5K around the walls of Jericho (Joshua 6), he could not pinpoint the exact moment the walls would fall. All he knew was that he had received instructions from God, and he was determined to lead with strength and follow directions, even if they seemed ridiculous.

Even Jesus had second thoughts in the Garden of Gethsemane (Matthew 26:39). But He had faith at 51 percent that no matter what suffering He had to endure on the path before Him, His Father would be faithful to the end.

One of my favorite Bible stories tells about a woman whose husband has died and left her with a tremendous debt she can't pay (2 Kings 4). The debt is so great that the people she owes have threatened to take her sons as slaves to repay it. She goes to Elisha for help, and he asks what she has in the house. All she has on hand is a small jar of oil. She is desperate—but then a miracle happens. Elisha directs her to borrow empty jars from all her neighbors and then to pour her oil into their jars. I'm sure she's thinking, *This is crazy.* But she musters up just enough faith to go along with it. She borrows so many big containers that they fill her whole house.

What happens next blows her mind, and it still blows mine. Get this: when she begins to pour out the remaining oil from her little jar, it multiplies and keeps flowing until she has filled every last borrowed vessel. Imagine this precious woman's 51 percent faith that gives her just enough humble assurance to knock on that first neighbor's door. She couldn't possibly be 100 percent sure that the little she has will multiply at all, let alone become enough to pay off all her debts! But what little assurance she has is enough for God.

> **GOD IS BIG ENOUGH TO HANDLE OUR QUESTIONS. HE IS NOT THREATENED OR INTIMIDATED BY THEM.**

In all these stories, there are details the Bible *doesn't* tell us—like exactly how much time went by or how many extra questions were asked or how many tears were shed before a step of 51 percent faith was taken. God is big enough to handle our questions. He is not threatened or intimidated by them. He does, however, want us to believe what He says. Sometimes He sends signs: physical, visible proof to help mitigate our unbelief. In other seasons, another believer's testimony can push us over the 50 percent mark.

If we can become just 51 percent confident that what He says is true, that's enough for us to keep moving in obedience and expectation and enough for God to create a new opportunity for the impossible to happen.

PLEASING GOD IS POSSIBLE

Hebrews 10:38 says, "My righteous ones will live by faith." For anyone who is a Christ follower and wants to be counted as righteous, living by faith is not an option. Sorry, not sorry. We can't make ourselves righteous; only God can. It is our privilege to be righteous examples of what God can do with unqualified, unrefined, and sometimes misunderstood people like you and me who believe beyond the borders of what is reasonable. Faith in God is not a suggestion or a recommendation. It's a command.

Further, Hebrews 11:6 tells us that without faith, it is impossible to please God. This scripture comes alive to me when I read it in reverse: *with* faith, pleasing God *is* possible. Sometimes we make this concept way too complicated, but it's that easy. My faith pleases God. Your faith pleases God. Our faith together pleases God.

We can't expect to please God if we don't believe in Him and what He says. If my kids didn't believe I'm real, didn't believe

> **LIVING BY FAITH IS NOT AN OPTION.**

that I care about them enough to provide for them, correct them, and comfort them, they would run wild all over the house, freak out about what they lack, and probably end up hurting themselves and others. This sounds a lot like what unbelievers do on a regular basis. And I don't mean only people who don't go to church. Even the church is full of unbelievers who are not convinced that all this stuff they hear in the Bible is really true. They don't have enough faith.

I get it. Bible stories can sound far-fetched to us today. You expect me to believe a Long John Silver's snack pack fed over five thousand hungry people? You expect me to believe an entire nation of people walked up to a sea and the water split a dry path down the middle for them to walk through, like they were at an aquarium? You mean to tell me a young farm boy with a measly slingshot went to battle with an armed warrior giant and *won*? Yes. Yes, I do! These stories are true, and the Word of God is full of them. And the best part is that stories like these are still being written through the faith-filled lives of people today. God didn't do His best work in the Bible days and then lay it all down to retire. He's still the same God with the same power.

You can't do anything without faith. According to Ephesians 2:8–9, you can't even accept salvation without faith. By implication, Matthew 21:22 says you can't receive an answer to prayer without faith. And you can't possibly live the abundant Christian life that is promised to us in John 10:10 without faith.

Faith is the foundation of any great move of God, but far too many people are trying to live without it. We can't receive the

> GOD DIDN'T DO HIS BEST WORK IN THE BIBLE DAYS AND THEN LAY IT ALL DOWN TO RETIRE. HE'S STILL THE SAME GOD WITH THE SAME POWER.

miracles, the life transformation, the wholeness, or the revival that God wants His people to experience until we level up in our faith. We've got to aim to please God, and the only way to do that is to have faith. Pleasing God is possible, practical, and purposeful.

It starts with baby faith. But then what?

INVISIBLE EVIDENCE

Have you ever tried to return something at a store but then realized when you got to the front of the line that you forgot the receipt? (This has happened to me more times than I can count. God bless stores that send virtual receipts to my online account so I can find them right there at the customer service desk.) Most retailers won't take returns if you can't present a receipt as proof that you actually purchased an item. If you're attempting to return something expensive from a high-end department store and don't have a receipt, I imagine the experience can get even more awkward and uncomfortable.

A receipt is tangible proof that a transaction has occurred. But what if I told you that God doesn't require tangible proof? God accepts invisible evidence.

Go with me here. Let's pretend for a moment that God is the owner of the highest-end department store in your city. You walk in to purchase a couple of items, and then when you go to the counter to check out, the clerk tells you someone has already paid for everything. To leave the store with the items you've chosen, all you have to do is show your receipt.

This is the moment when things could get awkward—but remember, God accepts invisible evidence. And your invisible receipt is faith, trusting something you cannot explicitly prove.

How would you feel if I told you that you could walk out of God's store with everything you have faith for? I don't know about you, but that's the moment when I would probably tell the clerk, "I'll be right back. I need to grab a few more things."

Faith shows the reality of what we hope for; it is the evidence of things we cannot see. (Hebrews 11:1)

Faith is our receipt, our invisible evidence. You can't see it, but you can believe it. You can believe for things that seem impossible, things that are currently intangible, things that are so big, they seem immeasurable. God simply requires you to have faith for Him to take care of the end result.

We cannot see God with our natural eyes, but invisible, intangible faith is proof of the invisible, intangible God in whom we trust. Our faith in God is itself evidence that He is real and able. If He were not, then we wouldn't even be here to have faith in Him in the first place!

Faith is having confidence in who God is. And let me tell you,

> EVEN A SMALL AMOUNT OF CONFIDENCE OPENS THE DOOR FOR YOU TO BEGIN BELIEVING THAT GOD CAN AND WILL DO EVEN GREATER GOOD FOR YOU, IN YOU, AND THROUGH YOU.

Father God responds to that confidence. What father doesn't like when his kids brag about him? Even a small amount of confidence opens the door for you to begin believing that God can and will do even greater good for you, in you, and through you.

Another translation of Hebrews 11:1 says, "Now faith is confidence in what we hope for and *assurance* about what we do not see" (NIV, emphasis added). If we really understood the authority that is given to us as believers, we would begin to pray with a level of faith that brings about assurance. Notice, I didn't say insurance but *assurance*. Insurance is something you pay into to restore assets or supplement income in the event that you experience a loss. It can't always restore everything that has been damaged, and it gives back to you only according to what you put into it.

Assurance, however, is a reliable truth outside yourself on which you can confidently depend. It's already purchased and is freely given to you.

I made Natalie my wife because I was 51 percent sure. I had no tangible evidence that everything would work out. All I had was invisible evidence, a.k.a. 𝕮𝖗𝖆𝖟𝖞 𝕱𝖆𝖎𝖙𝖍, and that was enough assurance for me to continue moving forward, trusting God's promise never to leave or give up on us (Deuteronomy 31:6). I don't want you thinking it happened overnight. My assurance continues to grow as I keep walking by faith. (It hasn't always been a smooth road. It's a journey with both peaks and valleys—okay, a lot of valleys. For the full story and all the juicy details, I refer you to my book *Relationship Goals*.)

Faith brings about assurance. It's not faith if you're depending on insurance that you paid for yourself. It's only faith when you find *assurance* in what Jesus already paid for you. And the crazy thing about it is, if you put your faith in Him, He will restore everything in ways you could never pay for on your own.

That's the level of faith we want to reach for—but how do we get from baby faith to steady, confident, unshakable assurance?

PROMISE > PAIN

Imagine with me for a moment that you are renting a nice house in the suburbs of your hometown where your favorite uncle and cousin live across the street, your parents live three blocks away, and your grandparents stay around the corner. One beautiful spring morning, you discover your landlady has taped a notice to your door. It politely informs you that she will be ending your lease in thirty days—but the good news is, she has another property already set up for you. She has even agreed to take care of all your moving expenses. It's the least she could do! All you're responsible for is packing up your family and your belongings.

The only problem is, the note doesn't tell you the new address.

What would you do?

In Genesis 12, this guy named Abram faces a similar situation. God tells him, "Leave your native country, your relatives, and your father's family, and go to the land that I will show you" (verse 1). God has not shown him the land yet, but He still wants Abram to go in faith. He doesn't tell Abram the name of the country, much less give him an address! Abram trusts the Lord and all, but this is quite a step of faith. "Go to the land that *I will* show you." The Lord is calling Abram away from his cushy comfort zone into the unknown so that He can unlock the greatness inside Abram.

No one has ever become great by staying comfortable. Like

Abram, you might have to walk away from that town where you grew up. If you're an introvert, it might be time to speak up. If you're the life of the party, it might be time to shut up. You might have to let go of the corporate position with all the great benefits. You may have to sell or give away some material possessions. You might even have to say goodbye to some people who were, at some point, your best friends. Stepping out in faith will make you leave what's familiar for what's uncomfortable. It will force you to be vulnerable and learn to rely on God as your provider instead of leaning on your own strength and resources.

But let this be an encouragement to you: the pain of faith is real, but it never outweighs the promises of faith. God's promises are always greater than the pain. If you keep reading Abram's story, you'll see that the very next thing God says after instructing him to leave his place of comfort is a promise to bless his socks off:

I will make you a great nation,
And I will bless you [abundantly],
And make your name great (exalted, distinguished);
And you shall be a blessing [a source of great good to
    others];

And I will bless (do good for, benefit) those who bless
    you,
And I will curse [that is, subject to My wrath and
    judgment] the one who curses (despises, dishonors,
    has contempt for) you.
And in you all the families (nations) of the earth will be
    blessed. (verses 2–3, AMP)

Guess what Abram does. He goes. And *as* he goes, God directs him and he is blessed, provided for, and protected every step of the way.

You'll find that God many times works like the voice guidance on your GPS: you don't get instruc-

> # GOD'S PROMISES ARE ALWAYS GREATER THAN THE PAIN.

tions until you start moving, and you get the next step just in time to obey it. God wants to meet you at the intersection of faith and obedience. You may have to sacrifice to step out on your faith and obey God. You may not be 100 percent sure it's going to work. But one thing I can guarantee is that obedience will prove much greater than your sacrifice. You don't know what you're being saved from and what you're being saved for—but God does. His plan for you far exceeds anything in your wildest dreams, but it depends on your willingness to trust Him and get going.

THE FAITH FORMULA

Call me crazy—you wouldn't be the first—but I believe God's greatest miracles are yet to come. I believe in Bible days He healed the blind, cast out demons, made a path in the middle of the sea, and pulled tax money out of a fish's mouth. But I also believe He said, "Greater works than these he will do" (John 14:12, NKJV). If Jesus had the audacity to have *that* level of faith in us, what is stopping us from believing we can do great things?

Too many believers are more interested in playing it safe

than in trusting God—and there is a big difference between claiming you have faith and actually living out a life of faith. I can show you with math:

$$\text{Intellectual Agreement} + \text{Trust} = \text{Faith}$$

> **THERE IS A BIG DIFFERENCE BETWEEN CLAIMING YOU HAVE FAITH AND ACTUALLY LIVING OUT A LIFE OF FAITH.**

Let me break it down for any of you who are feeling nervous because you just had a flashback to high school algebra. *Intellectual agreement* is knowledge that something is true, acquired through teaching and experience. *Trust*, however, is actually reliance on what you know is true. Unless you have both, you don't have *faith*. Intellectual agreement is a start, but on its own? Not faith.

Many people have trouble believing in God because He's invisible to our human eyes and intangible to our human skin. But no one doubts that wind is real. Wind blows, and we see its effects: a breeze rustling through our hair, a current rippling in a body of water, a sail expanding to carry a boat across, or a force spawning tornadoes, hurricanes, and monsoons that make tall trees bend and bow and that have the potential to cause massive destruction. We were taught in school that the name for this invisible power is wind, and most of us intellectually agree that wind is a real thing. But some people actually go so far as to *trust* the wind. Some fly kites at the park. Others put up windmills to generate electricity. Thrill seekers go hang gliding or parasailing. All of them are relying on what they know about the wind *to actually do something.*

Wi-Fi is also invisible and intangible, but we intellectually agree that it's real. Even more, most of us regularly tap into its power, trusting that when we tap that little symbol on our smartphone, we'll be able to connect to a local internet source. We trust that it's working as we scroll through websites and use our favorite apps without a second thought. We intellectually agree that Wi-Fi is real even though none of us has ever seen it, *and* we trust it by using our devices that are designed to harness its power.

Putting your faith in God is like putting your faith in wind and Wi-Fi. Just because you can't see Him doesn't mean He is any less real or powerful. You may not be able to physically touch Him, but you can feel the effects of His infinite love, experience His bountiful provision, and witness His breathtaking creation. If you've ever seen the sun setting on an ocean horizon, peered through a telescope at the stars, visited an aquarium or a zoo, or traveled a winding road up the side of a mountain, then you've seen some of His creative power. If you've ever read about Him in His Word or heard stories about the amazing things He has done, you have come to know some aspects of His character. This knowledge is intellectual agreement, and it's a great place to start. But it's only half the equation.

Try this: The chair you're sitting in right now is a symbol of God's will for your life. You have faith enough in that chair to relax and allow it to hold your weight. Why? Because you intellectually agree that chairs are designed to hold people up and you trust that knowledge by putting your weight on it. If there's a chair in the room and your legs are tired, you sit. Unlike Goldilocks, most of us don't test out a chair by cautiously sitting on the edge for a second and then jumping up to make sure it's not going to collapse. We intellectually agree, because of our own and others' experiences, that chairs are engineered to hold people's weight, and we trust that fact by sitting down.

Let me ask you an honest question. If you can trust the Wi-Fi provider and you can trust the chair manufacturer, why can't you trust the Wind Maker? Why can't you trust God?

My wife, Natalie, and I have been working toward the goal of living a healthier lifestyle, and part of measuring our progress involves a task neither of us looks forward to: weigh-ins. Stepping on the scale in the morning with that imaginary drumroll in the back of my mind sometimes builds more suspense than a Marvel movie! I admit, I've been more than a little hesitant at times to put my full weight on the scale, usually because I know I've been eating too much fast food and am not going to like the result I see. It is possible that Nat has caught me trying to balance on the edge—as though maybe if I don't fully commit, I won't be embarrassed. It's also possible we sometimes do the same with God. Are you too afraid to sit down and relax in God's will because you fear being embarrassed if He doesn't come through in the way you expect?

> **IF YOU DON'T TRUST GOD'S WORD ENOUGH TO *PUT YOUR WEIGHT ON IT*, THEN YOU DON'T ACTUALLY HAVE FAITH IN HIM.**

Too many believers intellectually agree that Jesus is God and that God can do miracles but then don't put their weight on that knowledge. Here comes the true test of faith. If you don't trust God's Word enough to *put your*

weight on it, then you don't actually have faith in Him. If you claim
to believe God gave you a vision
but you don't trust enough to act
on that knowledge, you aren't putting your weight on Him. That's
not faith.

Even when He shows us only
a part of the whole picture, God
wants us to trust what He has

> **WHEN WE FULLY LEAN INTO THE PROMISES OF GOD, IT BRINGS OUR CREATOR GLORY.**

shown us. We won't get to experience everything God has for
us until we put our weight on it and act. But it's not just for
your benefit: when you sit in that chair, it brings glory to the
person who created it because you are allowing his design to
accomplish what it was built to do. In the same way, when we
fully lean into the promises of God, it brings our Creator glory.

We have got to start trusting what the Bible says about
God and put our weight on the fact that He's trustworthy!
He's never broken a promise or lost a battle, and He never
will. He knows literally everything there is to know and leads
and guides us into all truth. He's a good Father who wants
what's best for His children and knows exactly what "best"
looks like for each of us. You can intellectually agree and
that's great, but when you trust, that's when you begin to find
out that He is unconditional love, the Prince of Peace, the
center of joy, and the source of all good and perfect things.
The more you learn about Him, the more you will want to
know. And the more you act on what you know, the easier it
will be for you to trust Him. Fifty-one percent is all it takes,
but each act of trust grows maybe faith into *yes, Lord!*

What am I really trying to say? Put your weight on it.

Write the vision. Put your weight on it.

Write that blog. Put your weight on it.
Host that meeting. Put your weight on it.
Create that presentation. Put your weight on it.
Visit that relative. Put your weight on it.
Post that video. Put your weight on it.
Invest in that stock. Put your weight on it.
Take that job offer. Put your weight on it.
Make that deposit. Put your weight on it.
Get that second opinion. Put your weight on it.
Have that difficult conversation. Put your weight on it.
Apologize. Put your weight on it.
Trust Him, and take that *maybe* step of faith.

4

WAITING FAITH

MIDDLE SCHOOL MIRACLES

Back when I was pursuing a completely different career, the idea of me being a full-time minister sounded absolutely crazy. Sometimes I still can't believe I'm the pastor of a thriving church in my hometown. Like, *I get to do this?* I want to tell you more about all this craziness to give you some context.

In 2015, when my wife and I were handed the McIntoshes' baton and commissioned to be the lead servants (a.k.a. pastors) of Transformation Church, we had about three hundred members faithfully attending—which was awesome—but God had the audacity to show me a bigger vision. And I was just crazy enough to believe Him.

One of the first crazy things I did was to write out a vision God gave me for a new building. We had just barely paid off a 33,000-square-foot converted grocery store in the hood of Tulsa, which was a miracle all on its own. And yet here I was, just thirty-seven days after becoming lead pastor, on my computer in my daughter's room one early morning, dreaming bigger.

I went all out. I typed up a laundry list of all I was believing

God to do for our church, which included purchasing a huge event center across town, debt free.

That morning wasn't the first time I drew up a dream. Back when I was in middle school, I heard the scripture in Habakkuk 2 that says, "Write the vision and make it plain" (verse 2, NKJV), so I started drawing Air Jordans. You may think that's silly, but even then I had the beginnings of **Crazy Faith**. When one shoe design finally went from my sketch pad to my feet, I started drawing another—which eventually made it onto my feet too.

> "WRITE THE VISION AND MAKE IT PLAIN."

I was a self-proclaimed prophetic artist.

I took time on my sketches. I made sure the lines were just so. I used rulers and protractors and a good eraser. I traced pictures from magazines to get each one right. Why? Because I wanted to present my very best to God. I didn't have money, but I used what I *did* have to keep working my faith muscle. And as vain as those shoes seem now, I believe God allowed middle school miracles to build my baby faith so that as a husband, father, and pastor, I could trust His word on anything and everything with a childlike assurance that He will provide.

By the time I was fifteen, I graduated from high-tops and told my dad I wanted an eight-thousand-dollar drum set. (Thank God for my parents! They never crushed my faith. Parents, hear me: just because *you* don't have the childlike trust to believe for something, do not tell your children it's impossible. Give them permission to dream. You might end up learning something.) I started dreaming and praying and drew an elaborate, detailed sketch of a custom drum kit. Not much later, my dad asked me for the money I had been saving in faith for my kit. He told me to get in the car for a road trip to Kansas City. Every mile, my anticipation grew because I had no idea what was happening. We pulled up to a building, went inside, . . . and there sat my brand-new, sparkling, gold-rimmed, eight-piece, custom-made drum set—the most beautiful thing I'd ever seen.

"Your faith produced that," Dad said.

Now I know what you're probably thinking: *Um, no, your parents produced that.* But here's the truth. My parents were broke! It was *my* faith that attracted the needed finances *through* them. They were not the source. They were a resource that God used to bring His promise to pass in His child's life. And the testimony of that miracle boosted their faith as well as mine.

That early 2015 morning in Bella's bedroom, it was plain as day to me that God Himself had inspired those earlier prophetic drawings of shoes, drum kits, and other blessings. And that assurance prompted me to start typing some truly crazy faith-filled declarations. This is the first thing I heard the Holy Spirit say: *The SpiritBank Event Center will be Transformation Church.*

I searched online for an image of the SpiritBank Event Center (SBEC) and then used my amateur graphic design skills to stick a Transformation Church logo on it. Below the photo I typed, "The SpiritBank Event Center will be Transformation Church. We will have a state-of-the-art facility." As if that wasn't crazy enough, I followed it with eleven more faith expectations. The SBEC sits at the back of a huge complex that houses a variety of businesses including salons, chiropractic offices, multiple restaurants, a university, and a military recruiting facility. I had faith to believe that we would have

- The SpiritBank Event Center will be Transformation Church.
- We will have a state-of-the-art facility.
- The Kidz Zone will be a place that draws students from around the world.
- Somebody is going to underwrite the whole thing.
- We will always be in abundance.
- The internship will have a facility and be year-round.
- Businesses will be started out of our church that are successful.
- We will have amazing relationships with all existing businesses and all major businesses to come.
- We will subdue, rule, and dominate in that area.
- Many businesspeople and their friends and family will come to Christ because we re-presented God to them for transformation in Christ.
- Equipping the body of Christ will happen in this facility continually.
- The church will be filled three times over every weekend.
- Major secular events will be held there that will pay abundantly for the expansion of the kingdom.

fruitful relationships of influence with all the existing businesses *and* that new, successful ventures would be launched
out of our church for the kingdom of God.

Then I added this: "Someone is going to underwrite the
whole thing."

God instructed me to get up every morning and pray and
then He would show me what to do next. So that's what I did.
For some reason God trusted me enough to drop this tremendous vision on my head and heart, and Natalie and I were
determined to step out in 𝕮𝖗𝖆𝖟𝖞 𝕱𝖆𝖎𝖙𝖍.

The massive moment that was about to unfold began on
sketch pads as a middle school miracle.

DON'T BELIEVE IN SECRET

Let me reiterate: *all of this was crazy.* You have to understand
where our church was when I made this list. In March 2015,
Nat and I had officially been pastoring for one month and
eight days. We didn't have even a fraction of the money we'd
need for a new building. We held a single weekly service at-
tended mostly by African Americans. The church had just
been handed to me, an African American young person, by
Bishop Gary McIntosh, a middle-aged white man. According
to statistical trends, when an organization like ours experiences a leadership transition, its attendance, giving, and par-
ticipation all tend to decrease for a season. If they eventually
level out—and that's a big *if*—the audience will become more
like the new leader (that is, young and African American).

Well, I had 𝕮𝖗𝖆𝖟𝖞 𝕱𝖆𝖎𝖙𝖍 to believe that God was going to
not only buck the statistical trends and sustain us financially
but also turn us into a multiethnic, multigenerational, multi-

plying, multicampus church. (We were *none of those* at the time. You should have heard the crickets when I announced that part of the vision to a sanctuary full of people who mostly looked like me.)

In retrospect, perhaps the craziest thing of all is that I honestly expected people to jump on my faith-fueled bandwagon, even though I'd never pastored a church, never been to seminary or studied theology, and certainly never purchased a building. All I had was a promise from God and assurance to trust Him—because, after all, everything I'd done up to that point was only because of Him. (Still true.)

And here's the craziest of crazy things: people jumped.

> IT'S EASY TO BELIEVE IN SECRET FOR SOMETHING GREAT, BUT IT TAKES TRUST TO TELL OTHER PEOPLE ABOUT A MIRACLE THAT HAS YET TO MATERIALIZE.

I told our family and executive staff about the church God wanted us to become, and together we prayed over the vision. We unified our language and began to inspire the members of our growing church to believe for an unlikely future. I could have kept the whole idea to myself, but by telling a handful of trusted people, I unlocked an even deeper level of faith. As we stepped out in **Crazy Faith** together, God showed Himself faithful, continuing to provide the resources we needed to sustain while gathering the right people to partner with the vision He'd given for our future. Whom do you need to share the vision God's given you with? Who's around you that would partner with you in faith to take a next step?

It's easy to believe in secret for something great, but it takes trust to tell other people about a miracle that has yet to materialize. When God gives you a vision and you brag on His ability to keep His promises, it reveals your trust in His faithfulness. It lets others in on the stages of your testimony so they can witness the evidence firsthand, as it happens in real time. Most of all, it gives people the opportunity to partner with your vision and rejoice with you when it becomes a reality. Then their faith is sparked to believe God for bigger things in their own lives.

Our church staff prayed about how and when and where we should acquire a new building, and the Holy Spirit kept telling me He'd already given the answer. The SpiritBank Event Center came up again and again in conversations with people inside and outside the church. So I finally pulled up the document from March 2015 on my computer and shared it with the staff. We were in agreement for a miracle. It didn't matter how much money we didn't have or how little (zero) experience I had with bank negotiations. We couldn't ignore the Lord's clear leading.

When I met with our banker and informed him that God had placed it on my heart to purchase the SpiritBank Event Center, he literally laughed out loud—but he was so inspired by my faith that he agreed to walk with us through the process.

In spite of all the odds stacked against us, we didn't let go of the vision. 𝕮𝖗𝖆𝖟𝖞 𝕱𝖆𝖎𝖙𝖍 prepares with expectation even in the face of opposition.

DON'T SETTLE FOR THE SNACK

My wife is a great cook, which works out, because I enjoy good food. I have a problem, though. When I'm hungry, I get impatient. Natalie has this way of announcing what she's going to prepare and then disappearing into the kitchen, leaving me, my taste buds, and my growling stomach to imagine how delicious it's going to be. It's this period of time—between her announcement and sitting down to eat what she has lovingly prepared—that tests my patience most.

The gap between promise and provision is the hard part.

It can be incredibly difficult to wait on something I need or want, but what helps is knowing that I trust my wife. If Natalie says she's making something, she's making something, period. Even though I can't taste it yet, it's coming—so I wait and prepare myself to receive it. I clear the table and set out plates, napkins, and silverware. I walk the kids to the bathroom sink to help them wash their hands. I imagine how good it's going to be and how satisfied I will feel sitting at the table with my family to enjoy what Natalie has prepared.

> ## THE GAP BETWEEN PROMISE AND PROVISION IS THE HARD PART.

Real talk, though: there have been a few times when I decided I was too hungry to wait, so I went out and got a snack while Nat was cooking dinner. Nothing major, just a drive-through sandwich or a bag of Doritos. But don't go thinking those empty calories satisfied me. Settling for a counterfeit version of the promise you're waiting for never does.

There will always be an area of your life with a gap that only faith in God can fill. And if you settle for filling it with other things, I guarantee you will always end up disappointed. To top it off, you could delay the promise even more. My friend, I know you're hungry—but don't settle. If the promise you have faith for is as great as God says it is, He will also grant you the grace to wait for His provision.

Instead of filling up on snacks that ruin my appetite or sitting idly in front of the TV waiting to be served, I have learned to ask Nat what I can do to help. If she doesn't need a hand in the kitchen, I spend time with our kids so she can focus and work in peace.

While you're waiting, wait on God. No, that's not a typo. *Wait* on God—as in, serve Him. Find ways to support someone else's vision. Be generous with what you've already been given. Volunteer in your local church or charitable organization. Meet a need that someone else has been praying for in faith. Yes, it's important to keep your own God-given vision in mind and prepare yourself to receive it, but you can also be a part of His provision for the steps of faith being taken around you every day. Waiting on God while you wait on His provision makes the gap easier to endure.

Have you considered that maybe God is allowing the gap to prepare you for the promise? My oldest daughter still has quite a few years before she can be trusted to drive a car. I'm absolutely willing to teach her when she's ready, but I wouldn't dare put her in that position before she is mature enough to handle it. That would be irresponsible of me as her father, and it could put her and others in great danger.

In the same way, Father God sometimes tests our patience to build our endurance, train us to handle what's coming, and teach us to trust fully in Him. We can have assurance that He will never

> **WAITING ON GOD WHILE YOU WAIT ON HIS PROVISION MAKES THE GAP EASIER TO ENDURE.**

leave us alone during the waiting period and that His grace will give us power and wisdom to balance patience with taking steps of faith.

> Three different times I begged the Lord to take [the thorn in my flesh] away. Each time he said, "My grace is all you need. My power works best in weakness." So now I am glad to boast about my weaknesses, so that the power of Christ can work through me. That's why I take pleasure in my weaknesses, and in the insults, hardships, persecutions, and troubles that I suffer for Christ. For when I am weak, then I am strong. (2 Corinthians 12:8–10)

DON'T MAKE A FALSE START

There is a difference between **Crazy Faith** and just plain crazy, and a big part of it—after being at least 51 percent sure it's God giving you the vision—is timing. As of the time I'm writing this book, the fastest man in the world is Jamaican sprinter Usain Bolt. His accomplishments thus far include holding world records in the 100- and 200-meter races and the 4×100-meter relay, earning eight Olympic gold medals, and winning eleven world championships.

In 2011, Bolt was in South Korea at the IAAF World Championships and was the favorite to win the 100-meter race. As he and seven others got set in their blocks, silence filled the arena as everyone anticipated the sound of the gunshot that would start the race. Milliseconds before the shot, Bolt began to run. And almost immediately he knew his false start had cost him the race. To his dismay (but not surprise), he was disqualified.

He had the opportunity, ability, and experience to win. The only thing he had wrong was the timing.

I want to share a story from the Old Testament that's a painfully perfect example of getting the vision right and the timing wrong.

In this story the two main characters are Saul, the king of Israel, who in my imagination has a kind of Chadwick Boseman / Black Panther warrior majesty, and Samuel, the prophet and priest of Israel, who to me is a three-hundred-year-old Morgan Freeman–type character. Together they are to lead God's people, Israel. The way it is supposed to work is that Samuel hears from God and tells Saul the instructions, then Saul has faith to follow the instructions and, by example, lead the Israelites to do the same.

Only in this story, it doesn't go down that way.

In 1 Samuel 13, we read that while Saul's army is fighting a war against Israel's enemy, the Philistines, the king panics waiting on God's promised victory. The situation gets pretty hairy—the Philistines call up three thousand chariots, six thousand chariot drivers, and "as many warriors as the grains of sand on the seashore" (verse 5)—and Saul gets impatient. "The men of Israel saw what a tight spot they were in; and because they were hard pressed by the enemy, they tried to hide in caves, thickets, rocks, holes, and cisterns" (verse 6).

Before you judge Saul, have you ever been in a tight spot? Have you ever been hard-pressed? Have you ever felt like your only option was to take matters into your own hands?

Saul had clear instructions: wait for Samuel at Gilgal for seven days. But the king looks around and sees his terrified army slipping away into the wilderness. Verse 7 says, "His men were trembling with fear." Sitting in that tight spot, hard-pressed by the enemy and surrounded by soldiers scared out of their minds, Saul can't bring himself to wait on God's provision even one minute longer. Instead of waiting for God's prophet (the way it is supposed to work), Saul makes a false start. "Bring me the burnt offering and the peace offerings!" he demands (verse 9).

The king offers the priestly sacrifice himself, finishing just in time for Samuel to roll up. And the prophet-priest lets Saul have it:

> "How foolish!" Samuel exclaimed. "You have not kept the command the LORD your God gave you. Had you kept it, the LORD would have established your kingdom over Israel forever. But now your kingdom must end, for the LORD has sought out a man after his own heart. The LORD has already appointed him to be the leader of his people, because you have not kept the LORD's command." (verses 13–14)

Merriam-Webster says *hasty* means "acting too quickly: overly eager or impatient." Is it possible Saul is just a little bit hasty? Yeah, and look what it costs him. Instead of his descendants sitting on Israel's throne forever (which is what God wanted), God is forced to appoint someone else (David) who will not make a false start but will trust His timing. In fact, David trusts God's timing so completely, so assuredly, that he refuses again and again to take Saul's life to gain the throne, even many years after Samuel had anointed him to be Israel's next king (1 Samuel 24, 26).

> **THE RIGHT THING IN THE WRONG TIMING IS A CURSE.**

Saul is disqualified from the purpose of God for his life because he is too hasty. Too often what we think is moving us forward in the moment is actually moving us backward, disqualifying us in the long run—not because it isn't the right thing but because it is the wrong timing. The right thing in the wrong timing is a curse. The pressure of that tight, hard-pressed spot produces panic instead of trust in Saul. What do tight spots produce in you?

Can you imagine what might have happened if Saul hadn't given in to hasty faith? What if he had the audacity to see his enemies advancing and his army slipping away and still say to himself, *Well, I guess that means God's gonna show up and do something that ain't never been done before. I'll just wait right here and see whom I can serve.*

FOMO / DON'T WASTE YOUR WAIT

Many times in my own life, I've had a Saul-like experience. I wanted control. I wanted to know details. I wanted God to move faster than He was. When I dissected it, the root of all my discontent and dissatisfaction was fear. You can be sure that if fear is the root, the fruit will be rotten. I had a fear of missing out, or FOMO. *Waiting* faith is the proper response to hard-pressed tight spots. But when we allow pressure, comparison, discontentment, or impatience to lead us, waiting faith turns to hasty faith.

Let's look at the differences between hasty faith FOMO and waiting faith FOMO:

Hasty Faith	**F**orgets **O**rders and **M**akes **O**ptions
Waiting Faith	**F**ollows **O**rders and **M**aintains **O**bedience

> ## YOU CAN BE SURE THAT IF FEAR IS THE ROOT, THE FRUIT WILL BE ROTTEN.

When you have hasty faith FOMO, you do not pay attention to the last instruction God gave you. You forget your orders, and instead of staying obedient, you make up your own options. You just "figure."

"I figured it was good for me to get into that relationship."

"I figured it was the right time to start that company."

"I figured it was my season to leave that church."

"I figured it was time for me to move to another city."

> ## DON'T WASTE YOUR WAIT.

If you look at the story in 1 Samuel 13, Saul "figures" he'll take matters into his own hands and do the burnt offering himself—a priestly duty that a king isn't anointed to handle. He has FOMO: he forgets his orders and makes options. I get it! Waiting is hard, especially when what seems hasty to God feels like good timing to you. There's a secret, though. We get stronger in the seasons when waiting sucks. Being hasty may be a habit for you, but I encourage you to destroy that pattern by learning to wait. Your faith depends on it. Don't waste your wait.

Let's not get tired of doing what is good. At just the right time we will reap a harvest of blessing if we don't give up. (Galatians 6:9)

| Hasty Faith | **F**eelings **O**ver **M**y **O**bedience |
| Waiting Faith | **F**aith **O**ver **M**y **O**pinion |

Can you imagine what Saul is feeling during the Philistines' siege? He's the very first king of Israel, the leader of thousands of soldiers, and is experiencing the immense pressure of the moment. He's probably overwhelmed, scared, insecure, doubtful, timid, anxious, and feeling a barrage of other emotions too. And in this moment, he allows the filter of his feelings to become the focus of his faith. His faith is no longer in what God had said. His focus is only on what he feels.

I'm going to tell you something your mother, husband, or BFF should have told you: your feelings are your worst leader. Feelings are God given and should be used as important indicators. But when you let your feelings lead you, it usually ends up making you forfeit something God had for you.

> **YOUR FEELINGS ARE YOUR WORST LEADER.**

When you're waiting on God, don't let your opinion void your faith. We all have opinions. We all have a way we wish it would happen. But when we trust that God is sovereign and He sees us, what seems right now like a delay may end up taking us to our destiny.

Hasty Faith	**F**umbles **O**bvious **M**oments **O**ften
Waiting Faith	**F**aithfully **O**btains **M**ore **O**il

When Samuel anoints Saul as Israel's first king, he pours oil on him. In the Bible, anointing oil represents God's approval—so when Samuel anoints Saul, he is placing God's approval on him to lead God's people. But anointing isn't enough. It has to be mixed with faithful obedience. God chooses Saul. Israel's king has the "it" factor; he is the man God wants to use. But because of his hasty faith FOMO, his decision not to wait on God is the beginning of a pattern in Saul's life that ultimately disqualifies him. God then places his anointing, or approval, on David.

> THE ONLY THING HARDER THAN WAITING ON GOD IS WISHING YOU WOULD HAVE.

Think about this: if Saul had been obedient, David would never have been needed. The revelation that could be found here is that you never want God to have FOMO. You never want the Creator to have to find one more obedient.

Don't be hasty. Don't be too quick. Don't make a false start. The only thing harder than waiting on God is wishing you would have.

DON'T BUY A KMART

There's always a gap between the promise and the provision. The gap between God's promise of the SpiritBank Event Center and His provision of Transformation Church's new home was *almost five years*. There were times I didn't want to wait on God's timing and almost made a false start.

Our church grew and so did our responsibilities. I kept praying but also got busy with the day-to-day responsibilities of being a husband, father, and pastor. I grew, our family grew, and our church began to grow—a lot. In the midst of busyness, I nearly forgot about the promise.

By 2018, between fifteen hundred and two thousand people of all races and ages were attending five weekend services.

Parking was a nightmare. We had lines of cars up and down the highway. The neighbors were complaining. There wasn't enough space for our children's ministry. The air conditioning couldn't cool the building with the huge number of people in it. (Not to mention, we prayed daily that the fire marshal wouldn't pay us a visit.) We were busting at the seams, and it was past time for expansion.

We were hard-pressed and in a tight spot.

In our tight spot we had two options, just like Saul. We could wait on God or try to take control and have a false start. I remember two distinct moments when we almost made false starts. The first time, I loaded up the church vans and took our small staff to a vacant Sears building. I can neither confirm nor deny whether we sneaked into the building to envision our church there (wink, wink). I was so uncomfortable in the spot we were in as a church and so ambitious to expand that we began to make plans to move forward. Thankfully, we were never able to make contact with the building's owner.

The second time we nearly made a false start, we almost purchased a Kmart. It was in a less-than-desirable location and had a low ceiling and tons of poles. (This was already an issue in our current building: if you got to church late, the only seats left were blocked by poles, which is an awkward thing to face during worship.) That Kmart was nothing like what I wanted, but more importantly, it was nothing like what God had promised. But it was available and we were capable. Thankfully, our team felt it would not be sustainable long term, so we walked away and waited.

Rather than giving in to panic or discouragement, we remembered God's instructions—and we trusted. We prayed like crazy, prepared ourselves as best we knew how, took small steps of faith together every chance we got, . . . and waited. We had faith. It was *waiting faith*.

My friend, God *will* give you the promise, but first you've got to have waiting faith. Don't panic. Trust. Be faithful with the little you have now. Serve His people. Wait on Him.

5

WAVY FAITH

FAITH TO GET OUT OF THE BOAT

There's a story for everyone in God's Word, and the best part is that it's all true. Digging in is like bingeing the craziest reality show *ever*. The characters are real people who lived on the same earth we do, who experienced real suffering and saw real miracles because of their faith in God.

Spend some time in the Word and you'll start to notice that the Bible doesn't highlight many stories of people who play it safe or just don't bother. You won't find this: "There was a woman who had been bleeding profusely for over twelve years. She heard Jesus was passing by, but she didn't feel like getting out of bed that day, so she stayed home." Or this: "A group of guys with a friend who was paralyzed and bedridden wanted to take him to see Jesus the healer, but the room was packed, so they gave up and went home." Or this: "A prophet of the Lord told a woman in need of a financial miracle to borrow jars from her neighbors, but she was nervous about what they would think of her, so she didn't ask."

We rarely talk about people who stay safe and dry in the boat. No, we talk about people who trust Jesus enough to get

> ## WE RARELY TALK ABOUT PEOPLE WHO STAY SAFE AND DRY IN THE BOAT.

their feet wet and walk on the water. We talk about people with what I like to call *wavy faith*.

In this chapter, we're going to get to know my personal favorite of Jesus's disciples: Peter. Now, I call Peter a gangster disciple because he tends to go back and forth across the line between showing radical obedience to God's instructions and doing crazy stuff on an adrenaline rush—stuff like slicing off a guy's ear. (Don't worry; Jesus immediately heals the man.) I identify with Peter a lot. He's not shy about speaking his mind or questioning things, and he deeply desires to be a ride-or-die follower of Jesus. When faced with the crazy decision whether to get off a boat in the middle of a storm, Peter is the only one of the disciples to have wavy faith.

Our story opens in Matthew 14, just after Jesus has accomplished one of His most famous miracles: multiplying a generous little boy's Filet-O-Fish and empowering His disciples to feed thousands of hungry families. Even after all the people have finished eating as much as they want, there are twelve big baskets of fish sandwiches left over!

Then Jesus tells His disciples to get on their boat and cross the lake; He'll catch up with them later. What the disciples don't know is that they are about to encounter a crazy storm that will test way more than their sailing skills.

IT MIGHT BE GOD

The twelve disciples pack up their belongings and set sail for the other side of the lake, just as they've done dozens of times before. They do this sort of thing all the time, so there's no reason to think following Jesus's instructions will be anything other than easy-peasy.

Just as they venture to the center of this body of water, however, the waves start to pick up and the wind starts to blow. Before long, their small wooden ship is being tossed back and forth in a furious storm. Giant waves are churning. Gale-force winds are howling. In the midst of all this stormy chaos, the disciples catch sight of a faint silhouette in the distance. *That can't possibly be a . . . person . . . in the middle of the lake?* Rather than trusting their own eyes (and remembering Jesus's promise to join them later), they freak out, reasoning that the best explanation for what they're seeing is obviously a ghost coming at them as they fight to gain control of the boat.

As the shadowy figure draws a little closer, however, a voice calls out, "Don't be afraid. I'm here!"—and immediately, gangster Peter recognizes Jesus.

"Lord, if it's really you," he shouts, "tell me to come to you, walking on the water" (verse 28).

It is, in fact, Jesus—in the flesh—and He tells Peter, "Yes, come" (verse 29).

So Peter steps out of the boat and walks on the water toward Jesus.

Yep, you read that right! *Peter walks on the surface of a lake toward the Lord.*

Let's stop and think about what Peter has just done. Everyone always wants to harp on Peter for taking his eyes off Jesus and sinking into the waves, but just for a moment, let's celebrate the fact that *Peter walks on water*. That's an incredible miracle that defies human logic. Do you remember when we talked about how chairs are designed to hold people's weight? Well, in case you don't know, the surface of water is not!

First Corinthians 13:12, remember, tells us that right now we see in a mirror dimly but later we'll see face to face, reminding us that we can't always trust the first impression of our perception. When the disciples first catch a glimpse of Jesus walking on the water, they are afraid. Jesus had never scared them before, but this time, under these circumstances, they are freaking out because He looks different. They are already a little on edge because they're on a boat in the middle of a bad storm, but the fact that Jesus is coming toward them in a different way than they are used to causes them not to recognize Him. The unfamiliar causes the disciples to act in fear instead of faith.

> **WE CAN'T ALWAYS TRUST THE FIRST IMPRESSION OF OUR PERCEPTION.**

Now, I have to point out that these twelve men have been walking with Jesus pretty much every day of their lives for the past two or three years, and they still don't recognize Him. Back in 2004, when Natalie and I had been dating for a few years, I bet I would have recognized her silhouette in a snowstorm! But I admit, it would be harder to believe it was her if she were levitating or doing something else I've never witnessed a human being do before. But even then, I wouldn't be able to look away.

Wavy faith examines before expressing. If you don't give unfamiliar situations in your life enough time to unfold, you might label something evil when it's actually of God. If you don't look long enough while filtering your perception through the Word of God, it's way too easy to prematurely mislabel. The way God appears to you and moves and performs miracles in the middle of a storm may look different than when you were on dry land. The way He manifests in your next season might not be the same as you've experienced before.

You remember I told you about almost buying a Kmart in the midst of being hard-pressed and in a tight spot (a.k.a. a storm)? My perception was that we were in a position that wouldn't allow us to advance. I was preaching five ser-

> **WAVY FAITH EXAMINES BEFORE EXPRESSING.**

vices, my staff was tired, and people were leaving because of traffic. It didn't feel like God. I could have started saying what I felt. Things like "I guess we're stuck here." "This is not going to work." "I guess God's not going to do what He showed me." I could've let my frustration in the storm make me speak doubt or death. I could've let my frustration label the storm prematurely.

But I know from experience that what looks like a setback may be a setup.

Up until that point in my leadership, when we needed something, it seemed like it almost immediately appeared. I got used to God coming through that way. But now God was challenging my faith. He was up to something way bigger than what I had ever experienced before. He was using an unfamiliar method to send me a message. I later found out the message was "I'm working while you're waiting." Can God use the unfamiliar to deepen your understanding? Are you restrained by routine? Or can you stay committed when it's not clear?

> ## IT'S TOO SOON TO TELL, BUT IT MIGHT BE GOD.

The disciples *think* they see a ghost that means them harm, but what they actually *see* is Jesus coming to help. Today you may lament what you think is a bad breakup, but in a few months, due to God's hand, you'll see that it's the best thing that never happened to you. You may think the denial and rejection you experienced when you presented your business plan was a setback, but soon you will see it was a setup for God to reveal Himself in a new way and use you to perform a miracle no one has ever seen before. Some of the things you think are bad right now might actually be God— you just can't see Him clearly because you're smack in the middle of a storm.

It's too soon to tell, but it might be God.

UNFAZED BY THE WAVES

Why does Jesus tell Peter to get out of his safe, sturdy boat? Does He want to put His beloved disciple in danger? In fact, why would Jesus tell the disciples to sail out on that lake at all? Doesn't He know there's a storm coming?

Let me tell you why Jesus is completely unfazed:

In the beginning the Word already existed.
The Word was with God,
and the Word was God.
He existed in the beginning with God.
God created everything through him,
and nothing was created except through him.

The Word gave life to everything that was created,
  and his life brought light to everyone.
The light shines in the darkness,
  and the darkness can never extinguish it. (John 1:1–5)

We proclaim to you the one who existed from the beginning, whom we have heard and seen. We saw him with our
own eyes and touched him with our own hands. He is the
Word of life. (1 John 1:1)

John, one of Jesus's other OG (original gangster) disciples,
wrote that. He was explaining that when God the Father created the universe, Jesus (a.k.a. the Word) was there. Jesus was
there when the very first molecules of water were formed
from one atom of oxygen and two atoms of hydrogen. They
came together *through* Him. He was the waiting Light of the
World the Father said to "let there be." Before He instructed
the disciples to set sail, He understood the nature and behavior of everything in creation, including storms and winds and
waves. As creator, He perceived the storm's inner structure in
ways that scientists have yet to discover even today.

In Mark 4 we find another story where Jesus tells the disciples to cross a lake in their boat and they encounter a fierce
storm (verses 35–41). In this case, however, Jesus is actually *in*
the boat with the terrified disciples—knocked out, sleeping
hard, snoring, and probably dreaming about heaven (I like to
think). High waves are crashing in and the boat is filling with
water, but there's Jesus: peacefully asleep with his head cradled
on a sopping-wet pillow. The disciples wake him up, shouting,
"Teacher, don't you care that we're going to drown?" (verse
38). Jesus yawns and stretches, then rebukes the wind and
commands the waves to be still—like you do when you're

> **WAVY FAITH BECOMES CRAZY FAITH WHEN IT'S EXPOSED TO GREATER FAITH.**

their creator. The storm stops just as suddenly as it had started. He turns to His stunned disciples, all casual, and says (I'm paraphrasing), "What's wrong with y'all? Do you *still* not have faith?"

This is how unbothered Jesus is by the storms that paralyze us with fear. He knows the exact velocity of the wind and how many drops of water just fell to the ground. He knows what the doctor's report says, and He knows how your body was formed and designed to function. He knows the root of all your family drama. He knows how much your bills cost and how much debt you still owe. And He's unfazed by all of it. Jesus rests calm in a situation that causes the disciples' adrenaline to rush because He's the one who made the wind and waves.

Our job is to rest in Him and stand in our authority as God's heirs:

> You have not received a spirit that makes you fearful slaves. Instead, you received God's Spirit when he adopted you as his own children. Now we call him, "Abba, Father." For his Spirit joins with our spirit to affirm that we are God's children. And since we are his children, we are his heirs. In fact, together with Christ we are heirs of God's glory. (Romans 8:15–17)

Have you ever watched behind-the-scenes footage of a horror movie? Once you see how much makeup and special-effects lighting and how many prosthetics and green screens are involved, the end product gets a lot less scary. Jesus was behind the scenes of creation. Even at its fiercest, He is its confident, caring master. And because He models that confidence as a leader, He becomes the faith-inspiring example Peter needs to step out of the boat.

Wavy faith becomes **Crazy Faith** when it's exposed to greater faith. What I mean is, the minute somebody sees her leader strolling out on the water, the safe boat she's in isn't good enough anymore. (This may be why you're frustrated settling for the boat you're in right now: you've been exposed to greater.) Once you've seen what God can do through someone you're following, you want Him to do the same through you! The moment Peter is exposed to Master-level wavy faith, he has to try it for himself. And for a moment, he too is unfazed by the waves.

SAFER VERSUS SAVIOR

For the eleven other disciples, staying in the boat seems logical and safe. After all, boats are built for the express purpose of helping people venture onto water without drowning, specifically engineered as a way to navigate through storms that's safer than, say, jumping into the raging sea. Reasonably, they put their faith in their boat.

When Peter decides to step out on wavy faith, I'm sure his bros are thinking he's more than a little crazy—until they see his crazy miracle take place before their very eyes! I can't help but think there could have been twelve of those miracles that day, but Peter is the only one who listens when Jesus says, "Come." The others don't have faith to get out of the boat.

But forget getting *out* of the boat for a minute; many people won't even get *into* the boat because they can't swim. It's not so much that they don't trust the boat. It's that they know they won't be able to save themselves if the boat sails into a storm. Think about the amazing adventures they miss out on because they fear not being able to be their own saviors! They may try to convince themselves and others that they're content standing around on the seashore, but down deep they wonder what they're missing and wish they could move beyond what's safe and comfortable.

People who don't know how they're going to save themselves won't even try to start the business. People who don't know how they'll control a relationship won't put themselves out on the sea of vulnerability. They won't be fully honest or transparent with their partners. They're more likely to have backup love-life preservers on the side.

Honestly, their fears are understandable. A man-made boat is not the safest place to be. What if it leaks? What if the sail rips or the mast breaks? What if a bigger boat comes along and attacks? What if there's a storm? So let's give all the disciples credit for at least following Jesus's initial instructions to set sail.

But Peter has something nobody else does in that moment: closer proximity to the One who can save him. Stepping out of that boat and into the waves is the safest place Peter can be. Why? *Because Jesus is there.* Anywhere the Savior is, is the safest place to be. Even when Peter gets distracted by the storm, allowing fear to consume his faith and beginning to drown, he is in close enough proximity to Jesus to be saved. Without hesitation, Jesus reaches in and pulls Peter out of the water.

ANYWHERE THE SAVIOR IS, IS THE SAFEST PLACE TO BE.

It is not our job to save ourselves. It's our job to trust wholeheartedly in the Savior of the world and get closer to Him. Walking with the Savior requires you to step out of what's safe, but when you do, He empowers you to walk on something that has never held anybody else up. He wants to empower you to be the first person in your family who stays married longer than five years. He wants to empower you with wisdom to invest your money and set up a legacy of wealth for your future great-grandchildren, even though your great-grandfather had a gambling problem and his descendants have struggled with a poverty mentality all their lives. It's not up to you to change the course of your life and your family and your business; it's up to the One who made the wind and the waves and you. Draw near to Him, because He is mighty to save.

Make this your confession: *Lord, if it's You, tell me to come to You on the water. Tell me to start believing You beyond my borders. Give me a vision that's bigger than I am so I can believe You for it. If it's You telling me to serve these people who can't pay me, I'll do it; I'm just a resource and You're the Source. If it's You telling me to apply for that scholarship that seems out of reach, I'll do it. If it's You telling me to open my heart and be honest with my estranged father, I'll do it. If You tell me to, I'll step out of this boat in faith and trust You to make a way.*

God calls us to get into the boat, but that's not all. He wants us to stay onboard only long enough to venture out a little deeper. He desires for us to exercise wavy faith in the One who walks on the water He created.

So here's my question: Are you going to stay where you think it's safer or put your trust in the Savior?

EXPORTED FOR GREAT EXPLOITS

Good, bad, or ugly, every circumstance in your life is either God-*used* or God-*sent*. God uses anything and everything to accomplish His ultimate purpose. But has it occurred to you that God may have actually sent you into that storm?

Some people talk about storms being a result of disobedience or distrust in God's plan, but what happens when we run into a storm because we *obeyed* His instructions? Maybe you're like Peter and He needed to get you into the middle of the lake so He could perform one of His greatest miracles through you. Maybe He wants to test your faith to see if you're ready for where He's ready to take you. Maybe this route is a necessary detour that feels terrible but is actually saving your life. Maybe learning to endure and press through this hardship is making you acknowledge your weaknesses and helping you grow stronger in faith and maturity. Maybe it's helping you acknowledge that you have no better choice but to fully rely on God. Maybe where you are is no longer suitable for where God wants to take you.

Maybe you need to be exported.

> GOOD, BAD, OR UGLY, EVERY CIRCUMSTANCE IN YOUR LIFE IS EITHER GOD-*USED* OR GOD-*SENT*.

As *Merriam-Webster* says, to *export* simply means "to carry or send . . . to some other place." When certain goods are in high demand, they are exported where they're needed most to be distributed to a wider audience of consumers.

Wavy faith makes you trust that you have been sent. If you're acting in obedience, you may not feel like your current job has anything to do with your ultimate purpose, but you're there because you've been exported. If you're acting in obedience, you may endure unfair treatment from your boss and feel overwhelmed in a storm of confusion all week long, but it doesn't change the fact that you were sent. Your kids may act rebellious and fail in their school-work right now, but you have been sent to that family as a stepparent. You have been sent to that neighborhood. You have been sent to that school. You have been sent to serve at that church.

You've been exported, and what looks like your biggest storm is about to become the setting for your greatest miracle.

Peter is empowered to walk on top of water *where he is sent*. God is a divine orchestrator. He puts circumstances in place, aligns people's paths, and schedules certain events for a greater purpose than we can see. Some storms are scheduled. Jesus has to get Peter out onto the lake. He has a purpose in mind when He tells the disciples to go on ahead without Him.

For God's purpose, the disciples need to be in deep water where all they have to rely on is faith. Sometimes God sends a storm to frustrate us into a place of humility so that we seek Him for the vision that will get us to our next step. Sometimes He sends a storm to help us realign our priorities and focus on what's really important. Sometimes He sends a storm to demonstrate His authority over wind and waves.

> **SOME STORMS ARE SCHEDULED.**

When you encounter a stormy situation, don't be quick to think it was the Enemy. Remember, the devil hasn't sent the disciples into a storm; Jesus has. But Jesus is also with them in the midst of the storm, and even when Peter begins to sink, he calls out for help and Jesus doesn't let him drown. Peter could stay on the boat instead and shout, "Hey, Jesus! Come get in this nice, sturdy boat with me!" But he chooses to step out of his safety zone because he trusts that his Savior won't lead him out there to drown.

If you're in the middle of a storm, step back and evaluate: *Did God send this? Did God export me into this? What does He want me to do or to do in me while I'm here?* If you feel yourself starting to drown, ask yourself, *Have I taken my eyes off Him? Was I listening to someone else's call? Did I send myself into this storm?* If Jesus sent you there, do you really think He's going to allow you to drown? No way! I often have to remind myself, *Mike, you didn't call yourself to be a pastor, bribe people to be a part of the church, or make up that* Crazy Faith *vision you wrote down. It was all sent. And where God sends, He always supplies.*

Be honest with yourself. Are you assuming you can summon Jesus instead of Him sending you? Too often we make our own plans and follow our own instructions, then ask Him to join us. We want Him to fit into our schedule and sign off on our ideas and align with our will—but that's not how faith works. Faith works when we believe for something that God desires for us. We must learn to trust that if He sends us, He will be with us and, even if it seems impossible, He will make a way.

DON'T STRIVE—STRIDE

Think about this: Jesus walks to the place where the disciples have rowed. The Bible tells us the guys cast off and then row all night until they encounter a storm and see Jesus coming toward them on the water. This timeline doesn't make sense to me. Do you mean to tell me Jesus somehow has time to shake hands with five thousand families as they're leaving to go home, hike up a mountainside by Himself, spend significant time in prayer, hike back down the mountain to the lake, and then walk through the waves to meet up with His boys around 3 a.m.? The disciples have a head start. They have twelve people rowing a boat. They don't have extra tasks to do or detours to take. So how does Jesus get to the same point in a fraction of the time?

Jesus strides while others are striving. The online *Oxford English Dictionary* says *stride* means to "walk with long, decisive steps in a specified direction." During His earthly ministry, Jesus walked everywhere He went. He was never in a hurry, caught rushing, or afraid He wouldn't make it to His next destination on time. Instead, He relied on the power of the eternal God within Him to get Him where and when He needed to go.

Too many people row (grind, hustle, strive) their way to the place God is walking. You may be frustrated because you think you have missed opportunities while God's had you in a season of consecration (that means being set apart from the crowd so He can get your full attention). But in reality you haven't missed a thing, because God's timing is always perfect.

While others around you are expending energy rowing in relationships, running down career paths, racing against contract terms, and losing pieces of themselves along the way, you can stride into the di-

> **YOU HAVEN'T MISSED A THING, BECAUSE GOD'S TIMING IS ALWAYS PERFECT.**

vine purpose God designed just for you. If you would spend more time getting vision in God's presence than on networking and trying to build your own success, He could open one door that would allow you to surpass the people rowing with all their might. They can't see they're using all their strength rowing on one side and they're going in circles.

Don't allow the Enemy's lies to cause you to drift out into the middle of the lake, rowing in circles and cycles of sin by yourself. You cannot deliver yourself out of addiction, no matter how hard you try. Trust me, I've been there. You need the Holy Spirit. It's God's will for you to be whole, healed, and set free from every wicked distraction to your faith, and He is able and willing to help you achieve *everything* that is in His will for your life. Be open to the steps of faith He asks you to take toward freedom, and keep your eyes on Him.

I want you to know that God is a restorer of lost time. He doesn't stop time; He *restores* time. He exists in eternity, so time is not a constraint for Him. This means it's not too late for you. What took others a long time to do on their own, God can bring to you in a moment.

> **GOD IS A RESTORER OF LOST TIME.**

When Peter sees Jesus in the waves, he says, "Lord, if it's You, tell me to come." (He takes time to ask before he jumps! That's waiting faith.*) He isn't 100 percent sure (maybe faith), but when he

---

* Remember our definition of crazy? "Marked by thought or action that lacks reason." Sometimes the crazy thing God tells you to do is stay—which means you'd better wait long enough to ask! We tend to believe it takes the greatest faith to leave a place, quit a job, or walk away from a person, but sometimes it takes even more faith to stay put. If Jesus had said, "No, stay on the boat," it would still have taken great faith for the disciples to trust His word, remain where they were, and wait for further instructions.

hears Jesus say, "Come," he takes a step (baby faith)—and before long, he is walking in wavy faith. It might be the easiest walk he's ever taken because a supernatural power is doing the hard part.

God is looking for someone who will say, "Lord, if this job is You, if this relationship is You, if this move is You, if writing this book is You, . . . then tell me to come." Our see-it-to-believe-it generation wants to have faith in a way that everyone around us will accept and follow and like. But God is calling for radical believers who care more about what He thinks than what others think. Everything that seems crazy but is God-ordained will happen—but be prepared for the fact that not everybody will agree or understand. Not everybody will be there to cosign or clap for it. You might have to say goodbye to some friends or opportunities when you step out and say, "God, this makes no sense to my human mind, but if You're saying it, I'm all in."

There was a day in the process of finding our new church home that I went all in. We were ending a tour of another horrible building, and our Realtor asked me how I felt. I looked him right in the eye and said, "Do you want me to be honest?" He reluctantly said yes. At the bottom of the elevators at the Cityplex Towers in Tulsa, Oklahoma, I told him, "This may sound crazy, but I have a word from God that the SpiritBank Event Center is Transformation Church. So don't call me again until it's the SpiritBank Event Center." He took a big gulp,

> YOU MAY FEEL LIKE YOU'RE STANDING ON THE EDGE OF THE BOAT WAITING FOR GOD, BUT HE'S OUT ON THE WATER WAITING FOR YOU.

and because he knew I was serious, he resolved to be persistent and call the property owners every week until the SBEC became available. I was so resolved that this was God's will for us that I decided to stop striving and looking for other places. We were going to walk into what God promised us, even if it took a lot longer than I wanted.

And just at the moment we became content in the pace of grace, we got the call that our new home was available. (I can't wait to tell you more about that later.)

I know the waves look intimidating, but you cannot experience this miracle until you walk toward Jesus. You may feel like you're standing on the edge of the boat waiting for God, but He's out on the water waiting for you. And He's right there, ready to catch you if you fall to fear or distraction.

It's always more about *who* we have faith in than *what* we have faith for. While you're stalling, trying to figure out all the little details associated with your next step, God is waiting for you to take a baby step in obedience to Him. You may be an analytical type and think, *I'll follow God if He tells me what I'm going to do, when it's going to happen, why it's a good idea, and how much it's going to cost.* But God is saying, *Okay, looks like we're gonna be here awhile. I'll just hold this door open until you decide you're ready to trust Me.*

> GOD IS OKAY WITH YOUR QUESTIONS. HE'S NOT THREATENED BY YOUR OBSTACLES. HE CAN HANDLE YOUR DOUBT . . . BUT HE RESPONDS TO YOUR FAITH.

Let me reiterate: God is okay with your questions. He's not threatened by your obstacles. He can handle your doubt . . . but He responds to your faith. The Bible says God is searching the earth, not for high IQs or amazing talents, but for faith (Luke 18:8). There's so much God wants to do on the earth, but He's waiting to respond to our faith.

PRAYER IS PREP WORK

Jesus was all human and all God. He came to earth from heaven, choosing to take on our human nature—so Jesus walking on water is just as much a miracle as Peter walking on water. In his natural state, Jesus would have been susceptible to drowning the same as anybody else, but He was divinely in touch with a supernatural power that graced Him to do the impossible.

That same power is available to you and me right here, right now. We just have to know how to access it.

After Jesus instructed the disciples to get in their boat and go ahead of Him to the other side, He withdrew from the others and went up on a mountainside by Himself. He didn't go up there to have some me time or to reflect on the awesome miracles He had done that day. He went up there to pray. He needed to recharge and refocus in the presence of His Father. He went alone, to a place where there were no distractions, because He was spiritually preparing to stand on what others drown in. Likewise, our steps of faith must always be bathed in prayer and practical preparation.

> HE WAS SPIRITUALLY PREPARING TO STAND ON WHAT OTHERS DROWN IN.

Not many people talk about this part of the miracle Jesus did that night, but I'm convinced it's significant. Jesus's level of prayer and preparation behind the scenes enabled Him not only to walk on water Himself but also to empower Peter to follow Him. Many believers are not spiritually prepared to get out of the boat and walk to the place Jesus is calling. I would go so far as to say that's part of the reason Peter started to sink. Beware of stepping out of the boat if you haven't prepared to step out of the boat.

Every miracle has an act of faith attached to it, but the responsibility to manifest that miracle is on God's shoulders. Don't worry! He's strong enough to handle it—and our posture must be to humbly recognize that we are not. In prayer, we remind our prideful flesh that God is sovereign and has all power, so we rely solely on Him. Pastor and evangelist Owen Carr said, "A day without prayer is a boast against God." It's saying, "Thanks, I've got it from here. I'll call on You the next time something in my life falls apart." We have got to wake up and come to grips with the fact that we are not now, nor have we ever been, independent of God. In fact, we are totally dependent upon Him! He's the reason our hearts beat around one hundred thousand times every day without our even thinking about it.

Prayer is the spiritual component missing from a lot of impossible situations. It's a sign that you know you can't do miracles on your own and that you have faith in the One who can. It softens your heart in ways you cannot see and dispatches invisible help to invade your situation. It helps you keep your eyes on Jesus so the wind and waves don't distract you and cause you to sink. It keeps you focused on the One who blessed you with that promotion when all the meetings and job duties keep trying to consume your time and overwhelm you. It reminds you who your number one relationship goal is when you start dating someone new and become infatuated and distracted.

You might think you're ready for a certain blessing, but the back side of that blessing will kick your

> **PRAYER IS THE LANGUAGE OF THE DEPENDENT. EVEN JESUS UNDERSTOOD THAT.**

butt because you can't handle all that's attached to it. That's why you've got to pray. You want to be ready when God sends you somewhere. You don't want to fold because you did not prepare in the previous season. If you're single, practice being in the presence of God while you're alone so that your character will be able to sustain the blessing of a spouse when you receive it. Make seeking God a part of your regular routine now in private so that one day you'll be ready to do what God asks you to do in front of an audience. God can give you divine strategies through prayer that you will never get by researching a topic and polling a group of people online. Prayer is the language of the dependent. Even Jesus understood that.

If you aren't used to praying, it's very simple. Talk to God. Be honest about where you are, and admit you need Him. Ask Him to be your captain, and He will lead and direct you into truth. Jesus doesn't say you won't encounter storms, but He does promise to be right there with you through any you face. Even if He didn't send them, He will use them to give you a testimony that will bring Him glory once you reach the other side.

Be sensitive to God's voice as your faith is sparked. Be

ready to do something, like Peter, that is outside your comfort zone. And be encouraged, because when you get a vision or a

Here are four keys you can use as a guide to WAVY prayer.

W: WITHDRAW

When you pray, withdraw. There are so many distractions in the world today, but that's not new. Even Jesus, the Son of God, had to intentionally get away from the noise. "Jesus often withdrew to lonely places and prayed" (Luke 5:16, NIV). You do this by making yourself still. Get alone in your room, a car, the shower. Set a meeting place. Turn your phone off. Quiet the world around you. Take note—Jesus didn't just get away from bad things. He had to put distance between Him and good things because He desired the God thing.

A: ASK

God knows every storm you're in, every storm you've been through, and every storm in your future. He knows, yet multiple times in the Bible, God instructs us to ask for what we need. "Ask, and it will be given to you; seek, and you will find; knock, and it will be opened to you" (Matthew 7:7, NKJV). There is nothing too big and nothing too small. Ask about your needs. Ask for what He wants. Ask for His will to be done in others. Ask if you should come. Remember, Peter *asks,* "If this is You, tell me to come." Asking is attractive to God.

word from God and you respond by stepping out of the boat in wavy faith, the Savior is already there.

V: VULNERABLE

God's intention from the beginning of creation was for us to be vulnerable with Him. Think about it. Adam and Eve were naked. There was nothing to hide. When we come to prayer, we should come with nothing to hide. We share our fears, our shame, our troubles, our hopes, our desires, and our dreams with God. We can be vulnerable where we are safe, and prayer is our safe place with God. A WAVY prayer is a vulnerable prayer. Water is not usually solid. But Peter's vulnerability to get out of the boat produced a miracle that the world had never seen. What if your vulnerability produces your victory? "My power works best in weakness" (2 Corinthians 12:9).

Y: YES

When we pray, we expect God to hear us and answer us. "We are confident that he hears us whenever we ask for anything that pleases him" (1 John 5:14). You may have never thought about this, but God expects the same thing. He expects us to hear Him and answer Him. And our answer should always be yes, even if it's to walk on water. Obedience is 𝕮𝖗𝖆𝖟𝖞 𝕱𝖆𝖎𝖙𝖍 in action. It's our yes. So, when you pray a WAVY prayer, be ready to respond.

6

LAZY FAITH

STAY WOKE

I have faith that you're ready to pursue the promises of God for your life with all the 𝕮𝖗𝖆𝖟𝖞 𝕱𝖆𝖎𝖙𝖍 you can muster. But if you're anything like me, even though a part of you is gung ho for anything God says, let's be honest: there's also a part that's content doing absolutely nothing but sitting on the couch to binge the newest thing on Netflix.

In this chapter, I want to talk to the version of you that jumps up and shouts, "Amen!" at the pastor on Sunday but on Monday doesn't feel like doing what it takes to see the breakthrough you were believing for yesterday. I want to address the part of you that procrastinates on priorities and does the minimum required to get by, the part that settles for less than God's best because you don't actually believe you can obtain it if you try. *That* part. The lazy faith part.

When He catches His disciples sleeping on the job, Jesus has to talk to that part of them. "There is a part of you that is eager, ready for anything in God," He says (again, I'm paraphrasing), "but there's another part that's as lazy as an old dog by the fire." Let me back up and set the scene for you (Luke 22:39–46). It's just two days before Passover, and Jesus knows by the Spirit that one of His disciples is about to betray Him, snitching to the powerful people who want to get rid of Him. He has just finished the emotional Last Supper and predicted that His beloved Peter will deny Him three times before morning.

As you can imagine, Jesus is exhausted and overwhelmed with the heavy weight of His purpose, so He asks His three closest friends—Peter, James, and John—to come with Him to the Garden of Gethsemane to pray. The Lord withdraws alone to a quiet place and cries out to God, "If there's any other way that humankind can be saved, please Father, let me know. But I really do want Your will to be done, so I surrender." He wipes blood, sweat, and tears from His face and heads back, only to find His three boys leaning on each other, drooling and snoring. "Could you not even stick it out with Me for one hour?" He exclaims in frustration.

To be real, I identify with Peter, James, and John in that moment. I freely admit I have fallen asleep when I was supposed to be doing something important like paying attention in school or helping someone I care about or watching a movie on date night with Natalie. I'm sure Peter tries to play it off the way I do, mumbling, "I was just resting my eyes, I heard you. Zzzzzz . . . zzzzzz . . ."

Jesus is relying on His closest friends to be present with Him in the brutal final hours of His life . . . and they allow their flesh to take them out. I can't help but wonder, What if Jesus had a special impartation just for them that night but they missed out for a catnap? God

> **IF YOU DON'T CONFRONT YOUR LAZY FAITH, YOU WILL END UP SLEEPING ON HIS PROMISES.**

has amazing things for you. But if you don't confront your lazy faith, you will end up sleeping on His promises.

SOMEONE'S WAITING ON YOU

Did you know you're the first version of the Bible some people read? They may be reluctant to pick up God's Word for themselves, but they can experience it coming to life right before their eyes when they encounter you. They read the book of Derrick to see the fruit of the Spirit on display. They study the book of Maria to see how she puts action to her faith and the book of LaTasha to understand how to overcome adversity and anchor your trust in God. Someone is waiting to read your life story.

At times it may seem like no one sees the work you put in, but God sees it all. (It's also possible the person who holds the keys to invest in your "next" is paying attention from afar and admiring your diligence.) While you build your relationship with God, work on your craft, and pump up your faith behind the scenes, God is building a platform with your name on it. My boy, the apostle Paul, put it like this: some people plant seeds and others water them, but God is the one who makes seeds grow (1 Corinthians 3:6–9). Never doubt for a minute that the seeds you are planting or watering will bear fruit.

> **YOU WON'T REACH THE PROMISE WITHOUT ENDURING THE PROCESS.**

The thing about seeds is, they start their journey in darkness, underground with no one to see. It's only once they are full grown that everyone admires them. But not only that, people can be nourished by the fruit they produce. Someone is hungry for the fruit of your labor. Someone's life depends on your faith-filled actions. But you won't reach the promise without enduring the process.

Future generations are depending on the fruit of your faith. If you're forty-nine years old and still dealing with anger issues tied to an experience you had at age ten, don't be surprised if you begin to see similar issues in your ten-year-old son's behavior. On the other hand, if you put action to your faith, begin to see a therapist, and get some godly accountability, you can experience freedom from your displaced pain *and* break generational curses in your family line.

From the time He created human beings, God commanded us to be fruitful and multiply—but He didn't just mean having a bunch of kids. He wants everything we do to prosper and all our seeds to grow and flourish and bear good fruit. So why are so many believers trying to flourish on the fruit of their laziness? Too often, we say we have big faith but have too little to show for it. We have the audacity to broadcast our dreams and post our visions all over social media and declare to our friends and family in faith what God has said would happen, but when it comes time to put in the work, we get lazy.

PROPHETIC WORK

The opposite of lazy faith is *active* faith. It's faith that moves when God says move. It's faith that figures it out. All of us receive instructions from God in some form or fashion, and each of us has areas where we lack faith to follow through on

> **EVERYBODY WANTS TO GET A PROPHETIC WORD, BUT MOST ARE TOO LAZY TO DO THE PROPHETIC WORK.**

those instructions. You may not always be passionate about the next faith step you need to take, but that doesn't mean you get a pass. You may not always be excited to perform the next duty on your to-do list, but that doesn't mean you can put it off. Sure, you can pray for God to increase your passion, but remember, He's looking for your faith.

Let me help you. Plenty of people start out passionate about the process, but when you check in with them a few months later, they haven't made any progress. Why? Because they lack the discipline to follow through. Others don't even start. They pray and beg God for vision, but then they're too lazy to pick up a pen when He's ready to download it. They want to lose weight but are too lazy to plan healthy meals, so they keep eating convenient foods that contribute to obesity and disease. They're eager for an intimate and satisfying marriage but are too lazy to go to counseling. They're hoping to own a successful business but are too lazy to maintain a budget (even though you can always find them camping out in line when the newest Apple product goes on sale). What if that overpriced coffee you buy every day and the seventeen Amazon orders you're waiting on are delaying God's promise to you?

Everybody wants to get a prophetic word, but most are too lazy to do the prophetic work. We want God to bless us with more, but we're too lazy to steward what He's already given us. Faith *is an action verb*. The Bible says in James 2:26, "Just as the body is dead without breath, so also faith is dead without good works." This warns us that lazy faith eventually becomes dead faith. No one wants that, but the truth is, people die every day without having acted on their faith.

I once heard the late, great evangelist Myles Munroe say that "the wealthiest place on earth . . . is the cemetery."* It's full of the most creative ideas, innovative inventions, cures for diseases, and life-giving solutions that never came to fruition because they left this earth buried inside people who were too lazy to embrace the process and become who God called them to be. None of us knows when we will draw our last breath or when Jesus will return for us, so we've got to give our very best efforts while we are here! Let's please the God who invests so much in us and encourage those we've been called to impact.

God's Word says faith by itself isn't enough. Unless it produces good deeds, *actions,* it is lifeless and useless. Too many believers are wandering through life like the living dead, carrying around unfulfilled dreams in Christian coffins. It's time for the body of Christ to wake up and pick up our work.

Doing your work is prophetic. When you work on the vision God has shown you in advance, it inspires and prepares you for your future. It helps you call your future into alignment and builds the discipline in you to maintain the blessing when it comes. Our God is God of stewardship. He watches what you do with what He's already given and examines your heart to ensure you're ready to handle what He wants to give you next. He gives you glimpses into the future through dreams and passions and visions and prophecy because He wants you to start doing the work *now* and praise Him like it's already done.

* Myles Munroe, "Wealthiest Place on Earth: The Cemetery," January 2, 2021, www.youtube.com/watch?v=SyLVziS3758.

DOING YOUR WORK IS PROPHETIC.

We've got to learn to love discipline as much as we desire its results!

Now when I say put in the work, I'm not talking about striving in your own strength to grind and make it happen. I mean working wholeheartedly as unto the Lord and doing whatever your hands find to do with all your might because you know God is watching your stewardship (Colossians 3:23; Ecclesiastes 9:10). Romans 4:5 says it best: "People are counted as righteous, not because of their work, but because of their faith in God who forgives sinners." God counts us righteous because of our faith. No amount of work could ever cleanse us in that way. *At the same time,* faith without works is dead. We have a responsibility to do something. It's time to put our money where our mouths are—or more accurately, to put our action where our faith is.

Prophetic work looks different for everybody. For some, it's doing something they haven't done yet.

For others, it's stopping what's prohibiting their growth in God.

Some people want to be everywhere doing everything, but God is trying to get them to stay in one place long enough for Him to develop them into who He wants them to be.

You might naturally be an introvert, but if God has called you to touch the world, your personality will have to submit to your purpose. You might be a free spirit and like to do things spontaneously, but if God has called you to lead a team of people with systems and structures, your personality will have to submit to your purpose. You may have the gifting to do a lot well, but if God is asking you in this season to become a master of one thing, your personality will have to submit to your purpose. You might be an amazing marketer and net-worker on social media, but if God is asking you to take an extended break from scrolling to reaffirm your identity in Him, your personality will have to submit to your purpose.

> ## YOUR PERSONALITY WILL HAVE TO SUBMIT TO YOUR PURPOSE.

Don't wait for your destiny; start establishing faithful discipline in your life now. You could be a gifted singer, but don't wait until a door opens for you to go on tour to establish healthy eating habits and get in shape. Start working out *now* in preparation. I know it's tough to give up what feels good now in exchange for a goal you can't see just yet, but I promise you—it's worth it. Don't sacrifice your future promise on the altar of your present preference.

FAITH THAT WON'T QUIT

One of my favorite Bible stories is the account of the guys who carry their paralyzed friend to Jesus. They find out Jesus is in town healing everybody of everything. Broken legs, withered hands, leprosy, diabetes, clogged sinuses, heart conditions, issues of blood—you name it, He's healing it!

You may be familiar with the story already, but hear me out: Christians need to learn to read between the lines to hear what the Bible *doesn't* say. There are so many details left out of this story, it allows my vivid imagination to run wild. I like to pretend, for example, that the paralyzed man's name is Jerome.

Jerome is insignificant to some people. He's probably

been overlooked and forgotten—yet his friends are determined to get him to Jesus. Lazy faith won't bring what seems
insignificant to Christ. It doesn't feel like we should bother
Him with something small, some-
thing that matters only to us. But
Jerome's friends have active faith.
They trust that his pain and brokenness matter to God. First Peter
5:7 says, "Cast all your anxiety on
him" (NIV). Why? "Because he
cares for you." *Cast* is an action
verb. It takes active faith to cast
your cares.

> LAZY FAITH
> WON'T BRING
> WHAT SEEMS
> INSIGNIFICANT
> TO CHRIST.

You may be avoiding taking some things to Jesus because
you don't think He cares, but it's just not true. If it's important to you, it's important to Jesus. And if something is prohibiting you from reaching your God-ordained destiny, you'd
better believe He wants to deliver you from it. You may have
been carrying it to friends or to the bar or to social media, but
I really hope you'll start carrying it to Jesus. *He cares for you.*

The Bible doesn't say if Jerome has faith for his own healing. I imagine he is pretty discouraged. He may doubt his
friends will come through for him or that Jesus can really heal
him. But it's not Jerome's faith that gets him in front of Jesus.
His friends act on *their* faith by using their physical muscles
and working as a team to carry him to the house where Jesus
is. (I'm not sure how far they had to carry this grown man,
but nothing in Bible times seems to be a short distance—either
way, they sure didn't have a car.) Lazy faith would leave Jerome at home, but active faith causes these guys to pick him
up and carry him. Do you know someone who's discouraged
in his current situation, who has counted himself out from

receiving a miracle? Are you willing, on the strength of your faith, to carry someone who doesn't have enough stamina to take baby faith steps on his own?

After all that walking and carrying, carrying and walking, the friends finally reach the house where Jesus is teaching and ministering. But now they face another dilemma: the house is packed. Crowds of people are jammed into the rooms, blocking all the windows and doorways. (Whew, it's got to be hot in there!) How would you feel if you exerted incredible effort to act on your faith and carry your friend all the way to Jesus, only to find when you get there that you can't get inside?

This reminds me of a time when my wife was pregnant and had a random (but extremely urgent) craving for the Cheesecake Factory cheesecake one morning. So I got up, got dressed, got in my car, and drove across town. Imagine my frustration when I arrived and saw a closed sign on the door. I could have taken the lazy way out and gone back home, but I wanted my beautiful baby mama to have her cheesecake. So I got back in my car and drove to a local twenty-four-hour diner.

> **IF IT'S IMPORTANT TO YOU, IT'S IMPORTANT TO JESUS.**

As believers, we have to learn to persevere, to keep trying even when the promise doesn't come as easily as we hoped. A few of us might carry Jerome all the way to the house, but when we saw that crowd, we'd shrug and say, "Well, at least we tried." That's lazy faith. Lazy faith thinks one attempt is adequate. But don't be lazy and allow the crowd that surrounds your promise to deter you from reaching for it! The obstacles you encounter on your way to access the promise are sometimes a test of your faith.

Maybe the crowd is curated.

Maybe God designed this struggle to strengthen you.

Maybe the setback has significance.

Maybe the obstacle is an opportunity in disguise.

> **LAZY FAITH THINKS ONE ATTEMPT IS ADEQUATE.**

Some of the obstacles you're up against right now are proof that you're exactly where you're *supposed* to be.

Keep moving forward.

You tried to start the business. You tried to forgive her and mend that relationship. You tried church. But if you truly believe there's something amazing waiting for you on the other side, one attempt is not adequate. If you knew everything you need is on the other side of a locked door, what would you do? I bet you'd work harder than you ever have to pick or break that lock or even to destroy the whole door!

And here's the thing: sometimes the strength you gain working so hard to kick down the door is what you needed all along. We tend to think that challenges come to sabotage our faith, but God uses challenges to fortify our faith and produce perseverance in us that will increase our stamina to finish strong. James 1:2–3 says, "Dear brothers and sisters, when troubles of any kind come your way, consider it an opportunity for great joy. For you know that when your faith is tested, your endurance has a chance to grow." Without endurance, we've failed even before we try.

Thankfully, Jerome's friends see the crowd not as a dead end but as a detour. I imagine they think to themselves, *God's going to have to do something* really *crazy now. He's going to have to go above and beyond for this miracle. It's a good thing we serve the God who does exceedingly above all we can ask, think, or even imagine* (Ephesians 3:20). Consider this: when we go above and beyond in our active faith, God chooses to top that!

I dare you to go back to some of the areas where you've tried before and try, try again. I know it seems silly to quote a nursery rhyme, but that little message is prophetic. You might need to go back to some relationships that failed and try, try again. You might need to revisit that idea that you threw away after it didn't work out the first time and try, try again.

> GOD USES CHALLENGES TO FORTIFY OUR FAITH AND PRODUCE PERSEVERANCE IN US THAT WILL INCREASE OUR STAMINA TO FINISH STRONG.

Transform that lazy faith into active faith. Carry what you've feared is insignificant to Christ, and watch Him work a miracle that blows your mind.

Say it with me: "I. Will. Not. Quit."

RIP OFF THE ROOF

Anybody else might assume the only way into the house is through the front door. And that *is* one way—but there's always an alternative. Active faith puts in the work to figure out another way.

What have you deemed impossible because the most obvious way is blocked? Well, I'm here to tell you, there's still the roof. It might cost you more and require more effort and make people stare at you like you're crazy. But how bad do you want it? How bad do you want to see restoration in your relationship with your siblings? How bad do you want to leave an inheritance for your kids' kids? How bad do you want your marriage to thrive? How bad do you want to see people's lives transformed because of your testimony? Aren't you tired of being on the ground when your miracle is so close to you? Are you willing to rip off the roof?

Jerome's healing depends on his friends' active faith. They look at each other and nod. They know what they have to do: find a ladder, climb up the side of a house belonging to a person they do not know, . . . and dig a hole in the roof. And we're not just talking about a little hole. No. It has to be big enough to fit a full-grown paralyzed man lying on a mat. This is a special ops mission!

Lazy faith doesn't dare rip off the roof. Ripping off the roof demands boldness and sacrifice, and laziness is neither bold nor sacrificial. It doesn't consider sacrificing for the healing others need. Active faith says, "Hand me the toolbox." These friends know they are signing up for a construction project because the owner of the house has not asked for a skylight. They count the cost and decide one man's healing is worth their sacrifice.

There's no way Jerome gets to see Jesus and receive healing unless his friends act on faith to do something that has not been done before. They decide their *why* is worth it. If you identify the right *why*, you'll work for it like crazy. And the opposite is also true: it's way too easy to quit when you have the wrong *why* or none at all.

> **IF YOU IDENTIFY THE RIGHT *WHY*, YOU'LL WORK FOR IT LIKE CRAZY.**

I love the promise of Philippians 2:13: "God is working in you, giving you the desire and the power to do what pleases him." Paul is saying that when we make a decision to follow Christ, we accept the responsibility to realign our priorities (our *why*) with His—but we don't accept that responsibility without divine help. When we continually surrender and allow God to replace our desires with His, we receive His power to do what pleases Him.

God's number one *why* is people. Human beings are His passion, and He has gone out of His way to pursue relationship with us since before the beginning of human history. It pleases Him to see people healed and whole and free. And because He is the Healer, the Deliverer, and the Redeemer, He empowers our efforts to connect people to His heart and restore them to purpose.

When our *why* aligns with His—watch out!

God is love. His Spirit lives in you, and the fruit of His Spirit is love. Just like faith, *love* is an action verb. When you boldly sacrifice so that a precious human being created in God's image can experience another level of His presence, you store up treasures in heaven worth far more than anything you could acquire on earth.

NO CREDIT, NO PROBLEM

When you read Jerome's story in Luke 5:18–25—yes, it's only eight verses long—you'll notice that the Bible never reveals the names of the men who have active faith for their friend's life-changing miracle. The Bible refers to them only as "some men" (verse 18). They have no names or fancy titles. Luke doesn't specify their race or class or socioeconomic status. We don't know if they were celebrities or bums. We don't hear one more word about them after the events of Jerome's incredible day.

Lazy faith wants credit for every ounce of effort. If some of us were in the shoes of "some men," we'd be posing on the rooftop like "Hey, y'all are putting this in the Bible, right? Make sure you spell my name right and tag me on the gram." I can't help but wonder, *If it were me, would I be okay with no one knowing my name? Or would I be boasting all over town about how I played a part in getting Jerome healed, even though Jesus was the one who did the heavy lifting?* As for "some men," however, I don't think they are concerned about getting their pictures in the local paper or getting tagged or whatever. It seems to me they are far more focused on helping their friend experience transformation and playing a part in his future testimony.

"Some men" are not only willing to work; they are willing to work without a guarantee of credit or acclaim. They volunteer to be ministers and attend to their paralyzed friend's needs. As a matter of fact, I keep referring to them as "friends," but the Bible doesn't actually say they are Jerome's crew. There's no specific indication that relationship or obligation is influencing them to act on their faith that day. All we know is that they do what needs to be done so that a hurting man can see Jesus and receive his healing.

> SOME OF THE THINGS GOD'S CALLING YOU TO DO MAY NOT BE SEEN BY OTHERS ON THIS SIDE OF HEAVEN.

Active faith gets credit in eternity. Some of the things God's calling you to do may not be seen by others on this side of heaven. The work you do behind the scenes may not be publicly recognized. That's why Colossians 3:23–24 says, "Work willingly at whatever you do, as though you were working for the Lord rather than for people. Remember that the Lord will give you an inheritance as your reward, and that the Master you are serving is Christ." Be content to serve Him.

We can all take a lesson from these nameless heroes of 𝕮𝖗𝖆𝖟𝖞 𝕱𝖆𝖎𝖙𝖍.

FAITH TO FIGURE IT OUT

Imagine being one of Jesus's followers who arrives early enough to get a good seat inside the house. You're intently listening and taking notes when suddenly you see dust particles drifting down. The ceiling starts to crack! You look up and squint: bright daylight is blazing through an expanding hole, and the silhouette of a man is outlined in the glare. You think, *These people must be crazy!* And you're right.

Lazy faith won't figure it out, but active faith won't settle. These men who bring their paralyzed friend to Jesus have faith enough to work a few math problems (carry the one) and make a few reassessments of the situation to get him to a place where Jesus can heal him. They put in actual, physical work by carrying Jerome on his mat all the way to this house, climbing onto the roof, digging a large hole in the roof, and then—get this—safely lowering his mat right in front of Jesus. Have you considered how much strength and endurance it takes to lower a grown man through a roof? Some folks have a hard time climbing a flight of stairs with a newborn baby. This is a full-grown man lying, a deadweight, on a mat.

I remember helping my friend move from a ground-floor

> LAZY FAITH WON'T FIGURE IT OUT, BUT ACTIVE FAITH WON'T SETTLE.

apartment to the second story and feeling overwhelmed as we worked to figure out a way to get the sectional sofa into the living room because it wouldn't fit through the front door. Mind you, we discovered it wouldn't fit through *after* we hauled it up a narrow stairwell and around a tight corner. After all that effort, I was ready to drop the couch and let it slide back down the stairs with me on it! Jerome should be glad I wasn't in the group, because my arms and abs might have just given up and dropped him. (In my defense, Jesus *is* about to heal him anyway.)

The men put in some challenging mental work by finding the spot on the roof directly over Jesus's head and rigging some kind of system to lower the paralyzed body of a grown man without injuring him even more. The story doesn't outline every step of their process, but talk about creative! It is rough. It may be ugly. They probably have some disagreements along the way. The solution they finally come up with may involve one dude holding another dude by his ankles or a long intricate pattern of robes and tunics tied together in Boy Scout knots to form a pulley. It may take hours. I assume they don't arrive at the house with tools and supplies, so they may have to leave Jerome outside and trek back to get some rope and a hammer and borrow a rickety ladder from a nearby neighbor.

I want us to get the full picture of how hard they have to work so that we can feel a sense of encouragement about the daunting tasks that lie before us.

Some of us make such lazy excuses, claiming God hasn't told us anything—when in reality, He's told us step 4, but we refuse to act in faith to figure out steps 1, 2, and 3. Again, God usually shows us either the mountaintop without the path or the path without the mountaintop. He wants us to exercise active faith to figure out the in-between and trust Him to empower us to complete the journey.

I pray this story challenges you to reconsider your lazy faith. I hope a righteous frustration is rising up in you that refuses to settle for the outcomes you're accustomed to. I hope that you're saying, "This can't be all God has for me" and that you're compelled to get up, grab your toolbox, and dig deeper to find out more of His awesome plan. I have no doubt that "some men" had divine help figuring out how to get Jerome onto and through the roof of that house. I believe the Spirit empowered them to do what seemed crazy. And I believe He will do the same for you.

FAITHFULNESS OVER FEELINGS

We've done all this talking about active faith and how effective it is, but the honest truth is, sometimes we just don't feel it. We feel discouraged because we haven't yet seen results. We feel frustrated with God's timing because people are rushing us. It's easy to end up feeling doubtful and unproductive when we've put in faith efforts but are still waiting on faith's effects.

Let me remind you of our definition of faith from Hebrews 11: it's the evidence of what we can't physically see. Faith is proof that what God has said will surely come to pass. I know what it looks like right now, but don't grow weary in your well-doing. Remain consistent in your active faith, and resist the urge to get lazy. Close your eyes for a moment, and envi-

> ## SPIRITUAL MATURITY PUTS FAITHFULNESS OVER FEELINGS.

sion a picture of the abundant life God has promised. What do you see? That faith-based image is evidence. Hold tightly to that picture, and remind yourself of it on a regular basis. Your first act of prophetic work could be to put up some physical signs around your house to refresh your memory about God's promises to you.

You probably won't feel the effects of the work right away. Lasting change takes discipline, and building discipline takes time. This is something I have to remind myself of all the time because I would much rather have instant results. But there's divine purpose in the process. I don't see the results of my workout today, but my resolve is to keep going to the gym. You may have given money or time or other resources in **Crazy Faith** and have yet to see the return, but resolve today to keep being generous. You may have stepped out of your safety zone to act in obedience to something God told you to do. Don't stop just because you can't yet see the whole picture.

Spiritual maturity puts faithfulness over feelings. It magnifies our resolve to become greater than the results we've seen so far. Lazy faith makes "I don't feel like it" excuses, but **Crazy Faith** says, "I know it even when I don't feel it." God's Word is true and potent, and the principles found in it can transform your life, but it doesn't consult your feelings before giving you instructions. The Word is full of great and precious promises, but it's also full of commands from the Most High God.

Be diligent in your work, and keep putting all you've learned into practice. The Bible says Father God is "a re-

warder of those who diligently seek Him"—emphasis on the
diligently (Hebrews 11:6, NKJV). Keep stewarding what God
has entrusted to you, and He *will* send more. Remind yourself
why you're putting your faith into action. Your *why* is so
much more important than the way you feel. If you believe,
act: do something to back it up. Remain consistent so you'll
be faithful and faith-filled. The more you trust God and apply
active faith to the vision He has given you, the more He will
trust you.

RUN THE PLAY

Every year on Super Bowl Sunday, we get together with my
parents, brothers, sisters-in-law, and all their kids in front of
somebody's big-screen TV with some good snacks and watch
the big game. There's usually a little bit of a divide in the
house, but you can bet we're all united if we're watching the
Dallas Cowboys. (Oklahoma doesn't have an NFL team, so
here you're either a Cowboys or a Chiefs fan.) We are die-
hard, high-energy Dallas fans who enjoy yelling at the screen
as if the players, referees, and coaches can actually hear us.

We love experiencing the annual contest between the two
greatest teams of the year, but the Super Bowl would not
come to pass each February without the hard work, dedication, perseverance, and endurance that each of those guys sac-
rifices the other 364 days of the year. By that point, they have
run countless thousands of drills and watched hundreds of
hours of footage, studying playbooks and strategies to help
them outrun and outsmart the other team.

Now imagine if after spending all those hours in practice,
they just stand around on the field when it comes time for the

> **CHURCH SERVICES ARE THE HUDDLE. ONCE WE WALK OUT THE DOORS AND ONTO THE FIELD, IT'S TIME TO RUN THE PLAY.**

big game. They get together in the huddle and hype each other up, jumping around, pushing each other, and yelling victory chants—but no one ever kicks off. It might be fun to watch for a few minutes, but eventually, the coaches, refs, and fans would be screaming from the sidelines and from home: "Run the play!"

That's what the church looks like: a bunch of people hyping each other up like "I know breakthrough is coming! I believe for a miracle! Preach, preacher!"

Now, if you know the play, run it!

If you have faith, show us!

If you believe the Word of God, it's high time to live the Word of God!

Way too many believers still think that our faith is only for display at church. It's not. Church services are the huddle. Once we walk out the doors and onto the field, it's time to run the play. The game is played wherever *you* are—at your office, on the movie set, in the courtroom, in the laboratory, on the work truck, at school, at the coffee shop, in the studio, and especially in your home.

Time to break out of the huddle where we think about what to do without actually doing it. God is looking for believers who will be about that action! When we selflessly act on our faith to help others get to Jesus, the whole room will stop to take notice.

7

TRADING FAITH

THE OTHER SIDE OF THE MAT

I want us to stay with the story of Jerome and "some men," but in this chapter let's look at it from Romey's side of the mat. (The Bible doesn't say, but let's assume he has a nickname.) Romey's friends' active faith has brought him to Jesus's feet, but that's as far as it can take him.

Let's recognize: that's pretty far! I imagine Romey's friends just showing up at his house unannounced had made his day, letting him know he's loved and cared for. But then they don't leave him there. They start doing some heavy lifting to take him from where he is to where Jesus is. The gospel writer Luke picks up the story after they lower Romey through the roof to Jesus's feet:

> Seeing their faith, Jesus said to the man, "Young man, your sins are forgiven." (Luke 5:20)

Jesus sees *their* faith—the faith of Romey's friends—and announces that Jerome, lying there all helpless on his mat, is forgiven of all his sins.

This is a good day so far! Not only have Romey's friends

shown up for him with active, tenacious, figure-it-out faith. Not only has he gotten to see with his own eyes the Teacher and Healer everyone's been talking about nonstop. But now Jerome finds out *his sins are forgiven.* If I were Romey, I'd be hyped for how this day has turned out. Like, *Take me home and put me to bed. I've had the best day ever, and I'll remember it for as long as I live.* Thanks to his friends' faith, Romey will never forget his encounter with Jesus.

You may find yourself in a similar place today. The active faith of your mama or your cousin or your childhood best friend is bearing fruit in you, having brought you to encounter Jesus through the grace and favor and kindness they prayed into your life. You have survived the paralyzing choices you've made along the way, mainly thanks to the faith others have had on your behalf.

That's certainly cause to be thankful! I hope you're hyped for how things have turned out and that you'll never forget to be grateful you got to see Jesus. But I believe you're about to find out, like Romey, that this day isn't over.

People who know me say I have the generosity of my father and the tenacity of my mother. This tenacity shows up in all kinds of ways in my life but especially in my faith. From a very young age, Mom taught me to hold on to the promises of God, declare what I believe, and stand firm in the midst of frustration. As I was on this journey of believing for Transformation Church's new home, there was a moment when I seemed to have forgotten what she taught me. But there's nothing like a heart-to-heart with your mommy! At a dark moment when it seemed like all hope was lost, Mom reminded me what I had written down on the 𝕮𝖗𝖆𝖟𝖞 𝕱𝖆𝖎𝖙𝖍 vision paper. As she began to speak those things out with faith, it was like an electric shock went through me. Every sentence was like a faith defibrillator, reviving my faith in what God had said.

That was exactly what I needed in that moment. That conversation got me back to maybe faith, and I was so grateful. As soon as I left that conversation, I knew my mom's faith had helped me get here, but to see the promise of God, I needed an upgrade on my own. I needed *trading faith*.

> **SOMEBODY ELSE'S FAITH MIGHT'VE BROUGHT YOU HERE, BUT IT'S TIME TO TRADE IT IN.**

Somebody else's faith might've brought you here, but it's time to trade it in.

MAKE THE EXCHANGE

Once it's between just him and the Lord, Jerome finds out that somebody else's faith ain't gonna get it done. Romey has to be the one to take a baby step of faith—maybe his first step ever—to get where he wants to go. He has to exchange the faith that brought him *here* for the faith that will take him *there*.

That may sound crazy. Today you may be successful in business. Today you may be at peace with your spouse and proud of your kids. Today you may have a scholarship to the college of your choice. Why on earth would you trade the faith that's brought you here, to this place of blessing, for anything else? If it's not broken, don't fix it, right?

I'll tell you why.

Because Jesus isn't done with His miracle. He wants to do more in Jerome's life—and in yours. In fact, Jesus wants to

> **GOD NEVER DOES SOMETHING ON THE OUTSIDE THAT HE HASN'T ALREADY DONE ON THE INSIDE.**

heal Romey's body to show that He has healed Romey's spirit.

This is an important principle to remember: God never does something on the outside that He hasn't already done on the inside. He's not going to dump a bunch of money (outside) on somebody who hasn't learned stewardship (inside). He's not going to amplify your voice to the nations (outside) until you learn to speak with godly tenderness, affection, and encouragement to your family (inside). He's not going to give authority over more employees and resources (outside) to someone who is still trying to hide an addiction (inside). There's an outside chance those things could happen on their own, but unless God has healed you on the inside, they are not an outside manifestation of His miracle in you.

When Jesus tells Jerome to stand up and walk, He does it to "prove to you that the Son of Man has the authority on earth to forgive sins" (Luke 5:24). He wants to show through Romey's body what He has already accomplished in Romey's heart and mind. That's Jesus's *why:* to heal people of outside hurt, injustice, poverty, and affliction as a demonstration of His authority over inward hurt, injustice, poverty, and affliction.

But.

However.

Be that as it may.

On this day, in this crowded house, in front of these people, Jesus wants to partner with Romey to demonstrate His authority over sin. For that to happen, Romey must trade the faith that brought him to this place of inner healing for the **Crazy Faith** to get up off his mat.

It's the same with you: God stands ready to heal and bless you *for the sake of others,* so that others can bear witness to His authority to save. Don't get it twisted. This is not prosperity gospel. God is not a genie, and we are not magicians or sorcerers trying to say the right incantation so He'll grant our wishes. I don't believe God operates that way, and I don't believe **Crazy Faith** does either.

When God does a miracle, He does it so people can get saved.

> **WHEN GOD DOES A MIRACLE, HE DOES IT SO PEOPLE CAN GET SAVED.**

HOPE OVER HATERS

Let's back up a few verses in Luke's gospel. Not everyone is clapping for Jesus or cheering for Jerome that day. Jesus tells Jerome that his sins are forgiven, and then

> the Pharisees and teachers of religious law said to themselves, "Who does he think he is? That's blasphemy! Only God can forgive sins!"
>
> Jesus knew what they were thinking, so he asked them, "Why do you question this in your hearts? Is it easier to say, 'Your sins are forgiven,' or 'Stand up and walk'? So I will prove to you that the Son of Man has the authority on earth to forgive sins." (verses 21–24)

I don't want to focus too much energy here on the Pharisees and teachers of the law (a.k.a. the haters), because if you're reading this book, there's a good chance you're past the point of wanting, like the haters, for there to be holes in Jesus's argument. You're not looking for holes; you're looking for help! You're sitting here like Jerome: Jesus in front, haters in back. If you're going to trade the faith that brought you *here* for faith that can take you *there,* you're going to have to hear the hate but hold on to hope.

Remember when we talked about hope in chapter 2? It's the fuel of faith. But it can be hard to hold on to hope when haters (they may actually be people who love you, but they don't have the same hope) are hating. They don't believe Jesus has already worked the miracle because they can't see it yet.

When you say, "God is calling me to step out and start this business," they say, "You ain't got no degree."

When you say, "God said my marriage will live and not die," they say, "Girl, drop that no-good man right now."

When you say, "God promised my father will recover from addiction," they say, "Bro, your daddy been drinking every day for thirty-seven years."

When you say, "I'm believing for my debts to be forgiven," they say, "Credit card companies never forget."

Here's Romey, lying on his mat and having his best day ever . . . but now the haters gonna hate. If he's paralyzed from the neck down, he can't even cover his ears. He just has to lie here and hear it. There's some good news, though: Jerome is lying here in the presence of God. And as long as he's in God's presence, there is hope. Haters may shout hate from the back, but there is hope because Jesus is up front.

> **HEAR THE HATE BUT HOLD ON TO HOPE.**

TRUST, TRY, TESTIFY

The reason Romey needs to hold on to hope is that Jesus is about to give him new instructions to do some things he may have never done before. This is what Jesus says: "Stand up, pick up your mat, and go home!" (verse 24).

If I were Jerome, I'd be thinking, *This dude has lost His mind.*

Does He not see that I'm paralyzed?

Does He not see how broken my family is?

Does He not see how depressed I am?

Does He not see how many times I've been rejected?

Does He not see that no one has ever believed in me?

Does He not see that I'm unqualified and unfit for what He's asking me to do?

When God calls us to do something we've never done before, something we've been too paralyzed to even consider in the past, it sounds crazy. That's because it is. Remember what *crazy* means? "Thought or action that lacks reason." When Jesus tells Romey to stand up, it is not a reasonable request. It is a command marked by a lack of logic. And if Romey just relies on the faith that got him this far, standing up is too crazy to consider. If, on the other hand, he has trading faith, he is ready to trust and try.

Proverbs 3:5 says, "Trust in the LORD with all your heart; do not depend on your own understanding." And in this moment, Romey has a choice: depend on his own understanding ("My body is paralyzed; I don't know if I can") or trust in the Lord ("Your sins are forgiven; stand up!"). When you try, you show where your trust is. The next verse in Proverbs says, "Seek his will in all you do, and he will show you which path to take" (verse 6). Romey doesn't know if he can stand up.

But he trusts enough to make the exchange—the faith that got him *here* for the faith that will get him *there*—and tries. That in itself is a miracle.

"Pick up your mat," is the second crazy instruction Jesus gives to Jerome.

At this point you might be wondering, *Why? Why not just let Romey leave his empty mat lying there on the floor? If the dude is standing up, he doesn't need it anymore! Let the man get on with this incredible day and the rest of his life.*

Romey's mat is his testimony, and you don't throw away your testimony. "I used to lie on this mat all day every day, strapped down by chains of paralyzing sin. The active faith of my friends brought me to Jesus, and then I traded their faith for some **Crazy Faith** of my own. He loosed my chains of inward sin and outward injury, and He can do the same for you."

My mat is my testimony, and I carry it with me wherever I go. I will never throw it away. Let me be H.O.T. (humble, open, and transparent). Every week at Transformation Church, I make sure to carry my mat, even with thousands of people watching. I share openly that for more than a decade, I was addicted to pornography. It controlled my actions. It skewed my view of others. It perverted my concept of love and romance. It encouraged actions that hurt people I loved and culminated in me cheating on the love of my life before we got married. Most importantly, it hindered me from hearing the Holy Spirit.

> WHEN YOU TRY, YOU SHOW WHERE YOUR TRUST IS.

Many people have tried to convince me over the years to

stop sharing so candidly about my past struggles. They say things like "People are going to think that you're still dealing with it." "They may think less of you." "It doesn't look good for a pastor to say these things." What they don't understand is that sharing my real testimony is my secret weapon for how I stay free. The Bible says there are two things we need to overcome the Enemy and temptation (Revelation 12:11). The first is the blood of the Lamb. This is what Jesus did on the cross when He died and shed His blood so that we could be forgiven of our sins. The second is the word of our own testimony. My story of weakness is my weapon. Your story of weakness is *your* weapon.

> WE'VE GOT TO LEAVE THE SIN BUT TAKE THE MAT.

Our God is looking for believers who won't throw away their testimony, who will roll it up and carry it with them everywhere they go. I've heard pastors say, "Just leave it all at the altar," but I believe we've got to leave the sin but take the mat. Romey left his brokenness in body and spirit lying there at Jesus's feet and took the story of his wholeness with him to testify. I left my brokenness in mind and spirit lying there at Jesus's feet and am taking the story of my wholeness with me to testify. And just like Romey and me, you need your mat to let other people know—to testify—that they can be free.

You need your mat to win the battles that lie ahead. When the Enemy comes with his sneaky suggestions, his devious reminders of the sinful, paralyzed people we used to be, we will defeat him with the word of our testimony because we didn't leave it lying there on the floor when Jesus healed us.

HOME IS WHERE THE TRANSFORMATION IS

"Stand up" means *trust* and *try*. "Pick up your mat" means *testify*. The third and final instruction Jesus gives to Jerome isn't "Turn up" or "Throw a party" or "Say thank you like your mama taught you." No, Jesus instructs Romey to . . . "Go home."

I hate to be the one to tell you, but when you trade in the faith that brought you *here* for 𝕮𝖗𝖆𝖟𝖞 𝕱𝖆𝖎𝖙𝖍 that can get you *there,* the first place God will tell you to go is where the people know best who you used to be. Why? Because that's where your *transformation* will show. (It's my favorite *t* word of all!) Romey's home is where they've fed him, dressed him, cleaned him up, toted him around, and listened to his bellyaching for years. They're tired. They're discouraged. And Romey's miracle is just as much theirs as it is his. Just imagine what their lives will be like from today on. Imagine how their own faith for what God can do in *them* will grow.

Where will it be most obvious that God is doing a miracle in your life, that you are really, for real, transformed? In the home where your sin and emotional paralysis have caused chaos and despair among your loved ones. At the job you hate where your attitude is nasty every minute of every day. On social media where you try to gain likes and attention instead of spreading love and intention. In the school drop-off line where you curse out your own kids and every other parent and teacher starting their day. At a hang with your so-called

> THE FIRST PLACE GOD WILL TELL YOU TO GO IS WHERE THE PEOPLE KNOW BEST WHO YOU USED TO BE.

friends who push substances and situationships in your face that are part of your past, not your future.

At some point, for His glory, God is going to require you to be put on display in front of the people that knew you in your crippled state. Think about the testimony that it would be for people who knew you needed a miracle for so long and now you've finally traded up to 𝕮𝖗𝖆𝖟𝖞 𝕱𝖆𝖎𝖙𝖍. God wants to show everybody what He can do through your life.

I went to Edison Preparatory School from sixth through twelfth grade. During my time at Edison, I had a friend named Kyle. Kyle and I played basketball together, cheated in class together, chased girls together, partied together, and graduated together. After high school, we lost touch and our lives went in two totally different directions. Though I was no angel, Kyle unfortunately got involved with heavy substance abuse that deteriorated the quality of his life and his relationships.

I occasionally thought about Kyle, but it was years before I saw him again. One day not long after becoming the pastor of Transformation Church, as I was standing up to tell my story, I scanned the audience and was shocked to lock eyes with Kyle, who was there with his mom. I felt immediately overwhelmed with a burden to unroll my mat and share my testimony. That day, I was extra raw, real, and unfiltered. I wanted Kyle to know that if God could heal me, He could heal him too. At the end of the service, I asked if anyone would like to enter into a loving relationship with Jesus Christ by faith. As I closed my eyes to pray, I asked all those who wanted to participate to raise their hands. If I'm honest, there was a knot in my stomach not because Kyle *had* to make that decision but because I knew what that decision had done for me—and I wanted that for him so badly. After church, I made a beeline to the third row. We hugged, screamed, and acted like we were back in the sixth grade again. After catching up a bit, Kyle told me, "I prayed that prayer today. Hearing your story helped me realize that I am not too broken for God to still make a masterpiece out of me."

If I had hidden my mat, Kyle might not have found Jesus that day. I wonder who is waiting on you to unroll yours.

I know people from different backgrounds, walks of life, and even different religions are reading this book. And at this point, I feel that same burden for you that I felt for Kyle. If you've never accepted Jesus Christ as your Lord and Savior, I want to give you that opportunity right now. This will take **Crazy Faith**, but it is the single greatest decision you could ever make. It transformed me from being a liar, a manipulator, a pornography addict, and someone who had darkness in my heart to being a man who is not perfect but *is* progressing. Religion tells you that you need to clean up, get your act together, and change your habits before you come to God. But God wants relationship with you *now*. If you give Him your heart, He will help you change your habits.

Romans 10:9 says, "If you openly declare that Jesus is Lord and believe in your heart that God raised him from the dead, you will be saved." If you want to be saved, say this prayer from your heart:

Lord, thank You for sending Jesus to die on the cross for all of my sins. Today, I acknowledge that I'm in need of a Savior—and I choose You. I repent from my old ways of living and commit to a new life following You. I believe You lived, died, and rose again with all power just for me, so today I give You my life. Change me. Renew me. Transform me. I'm Yours. In Jesus's name, amen.

If you just prayed that prayer, you are saved. "Anyone who belongs to Christ has become a new person. The old life is gone; a new life has begun!" (2 Corinthians 5:17). You just made the greatest decision of your life. Heaven is rejoicing and so am I! Where you spend eternity is secure because your name is in the Lamb's Book of Life.

In case you're wondering, you just experienced *trading faith*.

I AM THE EXCEPTION

Our God is a miracle worker, and He dwells inside human beings who are always in need of miracles. Everyone faces impossible situations that need a God intervention. Yet not everyone experiences the fullness of God's omnipotent power working on his behalf. Many times, it's because people lack faith to believe He can and will do something amazing for them, in them, or through them.

Crazy Faith makes you believe you can be the exception. What happened in another situation does not determine what happens in this one. Your perception of previous patterns is not an accurate indicator of your future possibilities. There's always an exception. Why can't it be you?

This is a declaration not of superiority but of distinction. I'm no *better than* anyone else, but I am *different from* everyone else. That means you can't look at them and decide what God wants to do with me. The distinction is not always in the

> I'M NO *BETTER THAN* ANYONE ELSE, BUT I AM DIFFERENT FROM EVERYONE ELSE.

experience; sometimes it's in the outcome. We may go through what others have gone through, but that doesn't automatically mean we will come out the same way they did. This is not a denial of norms but rather a belief that you don't have to be limited by them, governed by them, imprisoned by them, or defined by them. Why should you be crippled by someone else's injury? That may have been her story, but it does not have to be yours.

There's always an exception—but God makes exceptions only in response to faith. As a minister, I often hear people crying out, "Lord, why me?" when they find themselves in the middle of impossible situations. When I do, I challenge them to respond in faith and say, "Lord, why *not* me?" *If You're going to grant someone favor with that financial institution, why not me? If You're going to allow someone to be the last person accepted into that university, why not me? If You're going to heal someone of cancer, why not me? If You're going to restore someone from depression, why not my friend? If You're going to turn someone's heart, why not my father's? If someone's home is going to remain standing after the tornado, why not mine? If You're going to bring reconciliation to someone, why not to my family? Why not my city? Why not my business? Why not my relationships? Why not me?*

I believe this truth about exceptions because Daniel went into a lions' den and came out the next day to tell the tale. People don't usually do that, so in Daniel's case God made an exception.

Daniel could've easily asked, "God, why me?" when he was thrown to the lions. But instead, I like to think he thought, Why not *me to walk out unscathed?*

People don't go into fiery furnaces with their homeboys and come out burn free, smelling "so fresh and so clean, clean," but in the case of the three Hebrew boys God made an exception.

Women in their nineties with husbands who are even older don't get pregnant and give birth to healthy babies, but God made an exception for Sarah and Abraham.

Large bodies of water don't defy gravity and split down the middle, but when Moses accepted the call of God on his life and held up a stick in obedient faith, God made an exception.

City walls don't fall down when a group of people march around shouting and blowing on trumpets, but for Joshua and the Israelites God made an exception.

Teenage farm boys don't pick up rocks and knock out giants, but in David's case God made an exception.

Someone who was sold into slavery doesn't end up becoming the right-hand man to the king of an empire, but in Joseph's case, God made an exception.

One meal consisting of two fish and five loaves of bread doesn't feed five thousand families unless God makes an exception.

> OUR OMNIPOTENT GOD IS IN THE BUSINESS OF MAKING EXCEPTIONS— AND YOU, MY FRIEND, CAN BE ONE OF THEM.

Mortal men don't get crucified, lay dead and wrapped in a

sealed tomb, and three days later pop out with the keys to death, hell, and the grave like it's just another day at the office. But with Jesus God made an exception.

I could go on. A young Black music producer with no seminary training was probably the last candidate that an accomplished middle-aged white pastor would want to hand off his church to, but in my case God made an exception! Statistically speaking, churches led by young and inexperienced Black pastors aren't multiethnic, multigenerational congregations that undergo exponential growth in just six years, but for Transformation Church God made an exception. *Why not me?*

All these examples are still only touching the tip of the iceberg. Our omnipotent God is in the business of making exceptions—and you, my friend, can be one of them. In fact, I believe you already are! Take a moment right now to think back over your life and remember some seemingly impossible situations you've faced. Now look in the mirror and remind yourself, *I am the exception.* He's done it before, and He can do it again. He did it for Romey, He did it for me, and He can do it for you.

Say it out loud: "I am the exception."

8

FUGAZI FAITH

THAT'S SO FAKE

I call Natalie's mom, LaDana, my mother-in-love. Since I was fifteen years old, she has loved me as part of her family, and over the years, we've become good friends. We text and call and drop by each other's houses just to chat about random stuff, because that's what friends who are family do.

I want to tell you about a recent time when LaDana came by. I'm sitting at my kitchen table one day, and all of a sudden I hear this frantic knocking on the door—*boom-boom-boom-boom*. I open the door, and here's LaDana, breathless and about to come out of her skin. "Mom, what's up?" I ask, concerned that it's an emergency.

"Michael. Oh, God. Thank You, Jesus. Oh, God. Thank You, thank You, Jesus."

I'm like, "Mom, take a breath. Tell me what's happening."

She pulls out a letter and hands it to me. "Michael, I think God has answered my prayers."

I read the letter to find out what God has done. This is what it says: "Ms. LaDana Miller, you have just been awarded $100,000." Wow, that's a good start. Then it goes on: "Send us $700 today so that we can release your $100,000 immediately."

I look up at LaDana, hating to disappoint her. "Mom, anybody who has $100,000 doesn't need your $700. This is fugazi."

"It's what?" she asks, deflating like somebody popped her balloon.

"Fugazi. Fake. Counterfeit. False. Definitely not real. A scam."

If you're an English teacher or my book editor, you might be feeling annoyed right now. Fugazi *is* not *a word*. I know; I know! I know it's not a word you can find in the *Oxford English Dictionary* or on Merriam-Webster.com. You know where you can find it, though? Urbandictionary.com, the crowdsourced dictionary of American slang. And according to that well-respected, reliable academic source, *fugazi* means "fake, unauthentic, substandard."

My sweet mother-in-love was taken in by the kind of scam that has become so common nowadays: targeted to older adults and close but too good to be true. It made me so mad. It nearly broke my heart.

But it also got me thinking: What other fugazi things are common today? "Gold" chains, sure. That "designer" handbag that cost $17.99, most definitely. The hypebeast sneakers where the logo is just a little off, yeah. Some of y'all got a weave or a lace front that looks like it could be your own flowing hair but ain't. (Which is fine, by the way. You're beautiful.)

> FUGAZI MEANS "FAKE, UNAUTHENTIC, SUBSTANDARD."

And then I remembered watching a Netflix documentary about the Fyre Festival, which was sold to the famous and/or very rich by supermodels as the greatest and most exclusive music event of all time. Everybody who was anybody wanted to be there. It was going to be held on a private island in the Bahamas, and the pictures they published to drum up ticket sales showed private luxury bungalows, bottomless premium cocktails, and stuffed lobster dinners served oceanside by superfit servers wearing white gloves and not much else. Concertgoers who could afford the hefty price tag would get up close and personal with the biggest stars in pop, rock, and hip-hop (Ja Rule was one of the promoters), with plenty of opportunities to snap Insta selfies with other B- and C-list celebrities.

Only none of it was real. Everybody who ponied up to get down there found cheese sandwiches in foam boxes instead of gourmet meals on fine china and FEMA tents and damp beds instead of five-star villas. There was no medical care for those who needed it and not enough water for anyone. When people wanted to leave, they couldn't get transportation off the island; they were literally trapped. The Fyre Festival was closer to an episode of *Survivor* than to a once-in-a-lifetime music event.*

It was about as fugazi as it's possible to get.

What would that look like when it comes to our pursuit of 𝕮𝖗𝖆𝖟𝖞 𝕱𝖆𝖎𝖙𝖍?

* Joe Coscarelli and Melena Ryzik, "Fyre Festival, a Luxury Music Weekend, Crumbles in the Bahamas," *New York Times,* April 28, 2017, https://web.archive.org/web/20190220210519/https://www.nytimes.com/2017/04/28/arts/music/fyre-festival-ja-rule-bahamas.html.

HADES FAITH

In my experience, faith is rarely as fake as the Fyre Festival. Sure, there are actual scammers who try to get seven hundred dollars from unsuspecting people of faith. And it seems like every week there's a new "Pastor Michael Todd" on social media with my profile picture, asking people for money. (If you're getting hit up on Instagram, delete that guy who has my face. He's fugazi.)

Most of the time, though, fugazi faith is not that obvious. And because it's not obvious—in fact, a lot of times it looks and sounds a lot like the real thing—it's important for us to have some standards for figuring out real versus fake.

The first feature of fugazi faith, compared to 100 percent authenticated 𝕮𝖗𝖆𝖟𝖞 𝕱𝖆𝖎𝖙𝖍, is that hell isn't afraid of the fake stuff. In fact, demons themselves *have* the fake stuff. Did you know that hell has faith? Don't believe me? James 2:19 says, "You say you have faith, for you believe that there is one God. Good for you! Even the demons believe this." If we hope to defeat the powers of evil, sin, poverty, injustice, death, and hell in Jesus's name, our faith has to get so much crazier than what those powers already believe!

> "YOU SAY YOU HAVE FAITH, FOR YOU BELIEVE THAT THERE IS ONE GOD. GOOD FOR YOU! EVEN THE DEMONS BELIEVE THIS."

There's a crazy story recorded in Acts 19 about what happens when people try to go up against the powers of hell with fugazi faith. (Spoiler alert: it does not go well.) The seven sons of Sceva, a Jewish religious leader, are traveling from town to town casting out demons. When they come across a person possessed by an evil spirit, Sceva's sons say, "I command you in the name of Jesus, whom Paul preaches, to come out!" (verse 13).

Did you catch that? Sure, they speak the name of Jesus, claiming His authority over dark powers. But they aren't speaking from faith that *they* own! They're trying to borrow Paul's faith and get something done.

> One time when they tried it, the evil spirit replied, "I know Jesus, and I know Paul, but who are you?" Then the man with the evil spirit leaped on them, overpowered them, and attacked them with such violence that they fled from the house, naked and battered. (verses 15–16)

"Who are you?"

That's cold. Even for a demon.

I know Jesus, and I don't mess with the Son. I know Paul, and that cat scares the hell out of me. But I've never even heard of you. Your name has never come up at hell's water-cooler, not once. And believe me, if you had any authority whatsoever, we'd all know your name.

𝕮𝖗𝖆𝖟𝖞 𝕱𝖆𝖎𝖙𝖍 starts with a real and personal relationship with God. It cannot be borrowed. God help you if you start claiming, "My tuition will be paid for in Jesus's name, whom Pastor Mike preaches." That's faith you don't own. That's power you're not plugged into. And that kind of fugazi faith ends in disappointment. Sorry to say, my friend, you can't write faith checks against somebody else's account. You may not get your physical butt whupped by a demon like Sceva's sons did, but your thoughts and emotions will take a beatdown. Doubt will be even harder to overcome. Your heart may get hard against God because you

> YOU CAN'T WRITE
> FAITH CHECKS
> AGAINST
> SOMEBODY ELSE'S
> ACCOUNT.

feel like He didn't come through for you.

There is a progression to Christian faith—or, more accurately, there is *supposed* to be a progression. We all start at *acceptance*. We accept Jesus as our Savior and Lord and have faith that He fully accepts us by forgiving our sins and saving us from hell. That's not supposed to be the end of the story, but I'm sad to report that a lot of believers stop right there and never go further or deeper into what God has for them.

When you accept Jesus, you immediately gain *access* to the greatest gift humanity has ever been given: the Holy Spirit. The real and actual presence of God takes up residence in your life to guide and direct where God wants you to go. He gives you instructions. This is how Jesus described the Holy Spirit to His disciples:

> When the Spirit of truth comes, he will guide you into all truth. He will not speak on his own but will tell you what he has heard. He will tell you about the future. He will bring me glory by telling you whatever he receives from me. All that belongs to the Father is mine; this is why I said, "The Spirit will tell you whatever he receives from me." (John 16:13–15)

I don't know if you've ever thought about this, but not a drop of rain had fallen when Noah started building the ark. And yet he had enough **Crazy Faith** to act in what I call the "tension of until." He got to work not *because* God did something but *until* God did something. Take a note from Noah. Your faith is authenticated through the next step: *action*.

The next step of progress is *authority,* and it comes only after we have faith enough to move through acceptance, access, and action. Paul's authority is what Sceva's sons try to borrow, but they act without access or acceptance—and get beat the hell up. When Jesus sends out the disciples to announce the coming of His kingdom, they come back hyped because "even the demons obey us when we use your name!" (Luke 10:17). "Well, duh!" Jesus says:

> Look, I have given you authority over all the power of the enemy, and you can walk among snakes and scorpions and crush them. Nothing will injure you. (verse 19)

And Matthew 18 tells us that Jesus promises, "Whatever you bind on earth will be bound in heaven, and whatever you loose on earth will be loosed in heaven" (verse 18, NIV). That is authority!

And finally, the progression of faith is supposed to finish in *abundance.* Why did Jesus come? "I have come that they may have life, and that they may have it more abundantly" (John 10:10, NKJV). Abundance means overflow; it means you are blessed to be a blessing to others.

Ain't nothing fugazi about that. Hell had better run.

FAITH VERSUS OPTIMISM

The second feature of fugazi faith is that it has no owner. There's no *Who* to whom it is directed. Rather than faith, it's just a generic kind of optimism. "Everything will be okay in

> SHEER OPTIMISM TRIES TO LOOK ON THE BRIGHT SIDE WITHOUT LOOKING TO THE LIGHT, JESUS.

the end. If it's not okay, it's not the end. Things are looking up. Better days are just around the corner. Somehow it'll all work out."

Optimism is hopeful, which is not a bad start, but its hopefulness has no object, no focus. It tries to look on the bright side without looking to the Light, Jesus. 𝕮𝖗𝖆𝖟𝖞 𝕱𝖆𝖎𝖙𝖍, on the other hand, looks right at Jesus and won't look away.

Jesus spoke to the people once more and said, "I am the light of the world. If you follow me, you won't have to walk in darkness, because you will have the light that leads to life." (John 8:12)

Sister Martha, in a story recorded in John 11, is a prime example of someone who does not settle for fugazi faith. She and her sister, Mary, and her brother, Lazarus, open their home to the Lord and His disciples every time they roll through the town of Bethany. Over the years of Jesus's ministry, they've become His friends. And so when Lazarus falls ill, Martha and Mary don't mess around—they send a faith-filled message straight to Jesus, confident and assured that He can heal their brother. Only Jesus doesn't drop everything right then and make the trip to Bethany. He keeps doing what He's doing until a couple days later, when He decides the time is right to see what He can do for His boy Lazarus.

The only thing is, by that time Lazarus is dead.

Oh, boy. Martha is *not* happy. And she's gonna to let the

Lord know. She doesn't even wait for Him to get in the house; she goes out to get in His face.

> When Martha got word that Jesus was coming, she went to meet him. But Mary stayed in the house. Martha said to Jesus, "Lord, if only you had been here, my brother would not have died. But even now I know that God will give you whatever you ask." (John 11:20–22)

Martha is not flippantly optimistic. She's not just trying to look on the bright side. But she is assigning her hope and faith to Jesus. She's definitely disappointed that Jesus didn't come when she and Mary called, and she ain't shy about letting Him know. But she is also vocal about her faith in the midst of the pain.

"You didn't show up when I asked You to . . . *but even now.* Even now, when my brother is dead."

Even now, when my marriage is on life support.

Even now, when my job prospects look DOA.

Even now, when writer's block is killing me.

Even now, when my child is ripping my heart out.

Even now, when I just got evicted.

Even now, when the depression's so bad death feels like the best option. If you've ever been depressed, you know that things don't just start "looking up." Better days could be just around the corner, but depression doesn't let you see a way to get from here to there. Optimism has no power over depression (in fact, happy-clappy positivity often makes a depressed person feel even more hopeless).

Optimism says, "I think I'm going to get better."
Faith says, "By His stripes, I am healed" (Isaiah 53:5).

Optimism says, "I hope my marriage works out."
Faith says, "What God has joined together, let no one
  separate" (Mark 10:9).

Optimism says, "It'd be nice to feel less lonely."
Faith says, "Jesus is with me always, start to finish"
  (Matthew 28:20).

Optimism says, "Someday I won't be addicted to porn."
Faith says, "In Christ I am a new creation" (2 Corinthians
  5:17).

Optimism says, "I have enough money to get by."
Faith says, "My Father owns the cattle on a thousand
  hills" (Psalm 50:10) and "My God will supply all my
  needs" (Philippians 4:19).

Optimism throws hope against a wall to see what sticks,
but faith assigns it to Jesus.

> **OPTIMISM THROWS HOPE AGAINST A WALL TO SEE WHAT STICKS, BUT FAITH ASSIGNS IT TO JESUS.**

When Ava Rae, our second youngest, was two, she went through a long (it felt like forever) season of not sleeping through the night. Every night between 3 and 4 a.m., she would stand up in her crib and yell, "Whoever! Whoever!"

No she didn't. Of course she didn't.

My baby princess yelled, "Daddy! Daddy! Daddy!" And

she was *relentless*. She'd yell my name over and over and over and over until I came in to pick her up. I'd crack open the door, and that second, she'd stop yelling, her arms would go straight up, and she'd sigh in the sweetest, most relieved voice, "Daddyyyyyy."

> # THE UNIVERSE DOESN'T HAVE A NAME YOU CAN CALL. IT'S CREATED, JUST LIKE YOU.

Ava Rae was not optimistic. She had faith that her daddy would come when she called his name. Please stop saying things like "The universe is working things out." No. It really isn't. Isaiah 40 says, "The grass withers and the flowers fade, but the word of our God stands forever" (verse 8). The universe doesn't have a name you can call. It's created, just like you.

Instead, call on Jesus. "All things were made through Him, and without Him nothing was made that was made" (John 1:3, NKJV).

FAITH MADE COMPLETE

We talked a couple of chapters ago about the absolute necessity of getting active and doing the prophetic work of 𝕮𝖗𝖆𝖟𝖞 𝕱𝖆𝖎𝖙𝖍, and I don't want to rehash all of that here. (Go back and read "Lazy Faith" again if you need a refresher!) But I do want to remind us right now that God will do everything we can't do but nothing that we can. He's not going to write a budget for you and take charge of your out-of-control spending. He's not going to listen to your young kids tell long, boring stories so that when they're older they trust you with hard questions. He's not going to whisk you

> **GOD WILL DO EVERYTHING WE CAN'T DO BUT NOTHING THAT WE CAN.**

through time and space to an AA meeting.

𝕮𝖗𝖆𝖟𝖞 𝕱𝖆𝖎𝖙𝖍 trusts God to do His work and gets cracking on my own in the meantime. The third feature of fugazi faith, on the other hand, is that the fake stuff wants God to do His work *and* mine.

There's a story in Genesis 22 that may be disturbing the first time you read it, until you've studied enough to understand what's going on. (Reading the Bible can be like that sometimes. It's the only book that when you read it, it begins to read you.) This is a story about Abraham, whom we've met before in this book, and the events take place after God has fulfilled His promise to make Abraham and Sarah first-time parents at an extremely advanced age. Isaac is born and everything's good . . . except then Genesis 22 rolls around and God commands Abraham to offer Isaac as a burnt offering. Yeah, that's right. To make his only son—God given, long awaited, patiently expected, and now beloved—a human sacrifice.

It's enough to give us the creeps until we understand what's going on here. God is asking Abraham if he's willing to give back what God had given in the first place. The thing is, He doesn't want Abraham's son. He wants Abraham's heart. Fugazi faith says to God, "No way, You gave it to me; now it's mine." But look at what James says about Abraham's faith:

> Don't you remember that our ancestor Abraham was shown to be right with God by his actions when he offered his son Isaac on the altar? You see, his faith and his actions worked together. His actions made his faith complete. (2:21–22)

Fugazi faith is incomplete because it won't do its own work. And, James goes on, "faith without works is dead" (verse 26, NKJV).

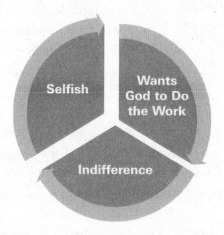

By contrast, faith doing its work is faith made complete.

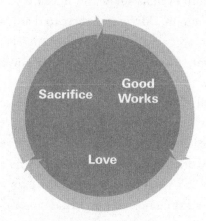

What exactly that work entails can change in its particulars—except for one detail. Paul said in Galatians 5 that when we have faith in Jesus, the specifics may vary from person to person and situation to situation. But, he said,

> ## LOVE IS FAITH DOING ITS WORK AND BEING MADE COMPLETE.

"What is important is faith expressing itself in love" (verse 6). Love is the constant. Love is the nonnegotiable. Love is faith doing its work and being made complete.

In a different letter, Paul wrote about the relationship between faith and love:

> If I had the gift of prophecy, and if I understood all of God's secret plans and possessed all knowledge, and if I had such faith that I could move mountains, but didn't love others, I would be nothing. (1 Corinthians 13:2)

Paul is reminding us here about Jesus's promise to His disciples. Do you remember reading about it in "Baby Faith"? "If you had faith even as small as a mustard seed, you could say to this mountain, 'Move from here to there,' and it would move" (Matthew 17:20). Moving mountains is pretty freaking spectacular, Paul says—but it's straight-up worthless without love.

Fugazi faith wants the results without the responsibility. It's a father who wants financial blessing to provide for his children while leaving the nurturing and affection to someone else. It's a coworker who wants courage to be a witness for Christ but doesn't want to hear about the pain of the person hurting in the next cubicle. It's an Instagram user who shares a meme against sex trafficking but has never donated to an organization that's actually doing something about it. It's a rowdy worshipper waving her hands around on Sunday morning and then spreading gossip at the beauty shop on Tuesday.

You might be asking, "How do I know that what I'm doing is love?" The most famous verse in the Bible is John 3:16: "This is how God loved the world: *He gave his one and only Son*" (emphasis added). So let me ask you this: What are you giving up in order to love? What are you sacrificing? What is your one and only?

Don't settle for fake, counterfeit, false, knock-off faith.

Work, love, and give so that 𝕮𝖗𝖆𝖟𝖞 𝕱𝖆𝖎𝖙𝖍 can be made complete in you.

I GOT THE KEYS, KEYS, KEYS

Although we were in waiting faith as a church, we were determined to make our faith complete by serving people while waiting on God to fulfill His promise. We were resolute: Transformation Church, no matter where we gathered for worship, would love the hurting, the broken, and each other, sharing the love of Christ with both the lost and the found. We sacrificed time, energy, and financial resources for others—in 2019, we gave away more than $700,000 to nonprofits, causes, and other churches' buildings. Our time had not yet come, but we were determined to keep sowing so that our harvest, when it was ready, would blow minds and change hearts. Our faith was not fugazi!

Brie Davis, Transformation's chief of staff, FaceTimed me on May 14, 2019. When I picked up, she didn't say a word; she just stared into the camera with excitement and joy over every inch of her face.

"What?" I demanded, but still she took her time.

"The owners of SpiritBank Event Center just called. They're wondering if we're still interested in the building."

My legs got weak, and the lights went dim.

The next thing I remember is driving across town with Brie and Transformation's COO and facilities manager. As I weaved in and out of traffic, I kept asking, "How? How is this possible? What happened? They were selling it to someone else!"

This is (of course) where an already crazy story gets crazier. An entertainment company out of Texas had been at the table to close the deal at 9:00 that morning—but at the last moment, their funding fell through and the deal went bust. Remember how our Realtor had promised to make weekly calls to SBEC's owners on our behalf? Well, his crazy persistence and our **Crazy Faith** kept us front and center in the owners' minds. So, when the deal fell through, they called us at 9:30.

I pulled up to SBEC, as I had done in **Crazy Faith** so many times before, but this time it felt different—like our prayers were coming to life in front of our eyes. Jim, the manager, asked, "Y'all want to see the building?"

With a lump in my throat I replied, "I want to see it *all*." And that's what we did. We walked every nook and cranny. It took more than three hours. And long before the tour was over, the four of us looked at each other and nodded. We knew this was home. By day's end we had put down $100,000 of nonrefundable earnest money and I was signing letter-of-intent documents.

I was still in shock the following week. I would wake up in the middle of night thinking, *Hold on. Wait. Did that just happen?*

A few days later, I got a call on my cell from a private number. It was a bigwig businessman from Texas who represented the entertainment company whose deal had fallen through. All their funding had now come in, and he said with incredi-

ble self-assurance, "I want to make you a deal you can't refuse."

It was maximum crazy. Like out-of-an-Al-Pacino-movie
crazy.

"Let's make this short and sweet," he said. "I'll give you
one million dollars to walk away and let us buy the building."

All I could see in my mind's eye was Dr. Evil from *Austin
Powers* saying, "One meeelllion dollarrrrsss," and I had to
swallow the giggles.

"No," I said firmly. I was almost as shocked as he was by
the confidence in my voice.

"Well, what about this?" he countered. "I know your
church needs the space, so what if I gave you a million dollars
and free use of the arena for five years?"

With a boldness I can't take credit for, I said, "Thank you,
but no sir. I believe we are supposed to own it."

He chuckled. "You drive a hard bargain. Here's my best
offer: free use of the arena for five years and *two* million dollars."

Two million dollars is a lot of money! My bold *No* almost
turned into a *Wellllllll* . . . But it was almost as if my certainty
and confidence grew in proportion to this gentleman's aggres-
sive insistence on acquiring the property. I *knew* we were supposed to own it for the kingdom of God. I politely declined a
third time and told him about the 𝕮𝖗𝖆𝖟𝖞 𝕱𝖆𝖎𝖙𝖍 journey we had
been on for almost five years. After hearing my testimony, he
knew there was no amount of money that could make us
walk away from God's promise.

My next call was to the bank president who had once
laughed when I shared with him my 𝕮𝖗𝖆𝖟𝖞 𝕱𝖆𝖎𝖙𝖍 vision of
owning the SBEC. "We're about to buy the building," I said.

"No way."

"We signed the intent papers last week."

"Wow!" he exclaimed. "What do you need from me?"

"Ten and a half million dollars."

"Done."

For ninety days we did our due diligence to make sure the building was in good shape, and on August 6, 2019, we purchased the SpiritBank Event Center—1,611 days after I sat down in Bella's room to write out the vision.

The wait wasn't wasted. We stepped out on a maybe. We didn't get hasty, and we committed to waiting. The journey was definitely wavy. But we stayed active and didn't get lazy. This moment proved our faith was complete, not fugazi. This miracle let me know I wasn't crazy.

That next Sunday, I stood on the platform, pulled the keys from my pocket, and announced, "I got the keys, keys, keys!" The faith and worship and joy that rose in that moment was like an electric shock through the whole room. (That's when I confirmed for myself that 𝕮𝖗𝖆𝖟𝖞 𝕱𝖆𝖎𝖙𝖍 is contagious!) Right then and there, I said, "We started in 𝕮𝖗𝖆𝖟𝖞 𝕱𝖆𝖎𝖙𝖍, so let's continue in 𝕮𝖗𝖆𝖟𝖞 𝕱𝖆𝖎𝖙𝖍. We are going to pay our new building off in less than a year!" And we all went a little crazy.

We paid it off in full and burned the mortgage on February 9, 2020—just five months later.

Don't tell me what God can't do. Don't tell me God doesn't speak. Don't tell me God won't provide. I'm living proof that none of those things are true.

It's only crazy until it happens.

9

STATING FAITH

USE YOUR WORDS

When an infant or a toddler wants or needs something, he grunts, whines, or cries. Occasionally he just makes demanding gestures or points in the approximate direction of whatever he wants until an adult figures out what he means and gives it to him (God help the adult who refuses). Babies are in the process of learning how to control their mouths to make sounds and form syllables, so they can't be expected to effectively communicate what they need in clear, well-reasoned sentences.

When they're still developing, sure, I can tolerate my kids throwing a few fits and making noises and pointing, but I don't want them to still be doing so at age twenty-five when they're ordering dinner at a restaurant. I want them to know it's not enough to reach or point or scream: you've got to use your words. The apostle Paul writes in 1 Corinthians 13:11, "When I was a child, I spoke and thought and reasoned as a child. But when I grew up, I put away childish things."

Nat and I do our best to teach our four beautiful kids to use their words to explain to us what they want and need. Their teachers utilize various methods to help them learn

> HE'S OMNISCIENT, SO HE ALREADY KNOWS WHAT WE NEED BEFORE WE SAY A WORD — BUT HE STILL WANTS TO HEAR FROM US.

clear, simple phrases when they want more juice or need to go potty. We all work together to help them grow up and clearly state what's on their minds. We often know exactly what they're trying to say before they say it, but we want them to learn effective communication, so we wait to respond until they ask. I believe this is how Father God sometimes parents us. He's omniscient, so He already knows what we need before we say a word—but He still wants to hear from us. He still wants to commune with us in prayer, and He loves to hear our voices lifted in praise and expressions of worship.

My only son, Michael Jr., was diagnosed with autism in 2018 when he was two and a half years old. Some of the challenges he faces because of autism are insomnia, light and sound sensitivity, delayed social development, and a lack of verbal skills. MJ is six years old, and currently words are still few and far between. As you probably can imagine, that has made it extremely difficult for his parents and caregivers to know how best to help him. Nowadays we've gotten much better at knowing his body language and deciphering whether he's hollering because he's upset, overstimulated, or just excited and happy, but it's still hard sometimes to know exactly what he needs.

Anyone who has the pleasure of spending time with MJ can see that he's both brilliant and resilient, and we thank God for the miracle in progress in his life. My wife and I have taken a stand in Crazy Faith, trusting God for his total wholeness. Part of our journey of faith with our little hero involves us sacrificing to take him to advanced therapy sessions where experts spend concentrated time and effort helping him to develop better communication skills. One phrase they and we use all the time is "Use your words." We're extraordinarily proud of his progress. You don't even know how thrilled we were when MJ started to point and use basic words! We praise him and give him tons of positive reinforcement any time he uses his words to communicate with us.

I want to encourage you: if you're having trouble with *stating* faith, just as I tell MJ, use your words. Perhaps it's a foreign language that you were never taught, or maybe some discouragement, distraction, or disorder in your life is prohibiting you from being able to clearly communicate to your Father what you need. But just as my son is learning, you can too! Remember, God is looking for progression, not perfection, and He wants to use different tools and teaching methods to help you expand your faith vocabulary.

It's not **Crazy Faith** until you start *stating faith*. When you start saying what you're believing God for out loud, it puts a demand on heaven and establishes a higher level of accountability with anyone who hears you say it. You can hope with all your might that something will work out; you can hold it in your heart and meditate on it day and night—but until you let it escape your mouth, it won't have as much power. All the good vibes and positive energy in the

> ALL THE GOOD VIBES AND POSITIVE ENERGY IN THE UNIVERSE AIN'T GOT NOTHING ON THE POWER OF YOUR WORDS SPOKEN IN FAITH.

universe ain't got nothing on the power of your words spoken in faith.

FAITH-FILLED DECLARATIONS

He made heaven and earth,
    the sea, and everything in them.
He keeps every promise forever. (Psalm 146:6)

Words are so powerful that they are the tool God used to create the entire universe. In Genesis, God spoke. He said, "Let there be," and whatever He spoke happened, just like *that*. Stars hung in the sky, darkness transitioned to light, seas cascaded across the earth, mountains formed, vegetation sprouted from the ground, fish swam, and birds flew. Words have creative power—and God chose to give that same power to you and me.

According to Proverbs 18:21, the power of life and death lies not in your thoughts but in your *tongue*. And remember, faith comes by hearing (Romans 10:17). As you echo faith-filled words that are based on God's Word, your own ears are the first to hear and receive them. When you speak the truth, your faith grows. The moment you start speaking the answer out loud, the worry and doubt that have tried to consume your mind begin to burn away as your faith is kindled into flame.

I want you to tap into that God-given faith-visualization tool of yours again (your imagination, remember?). Get a picture in your mind of something you are believing God to manifest in your life. I'm picturing my son, MJ, confidently standing up in front of his fourth-grade class to give a presentation that he completed all by himself. What do you see? What do you hear? What prayer has God answered in the future you envision?

Now as you exercise your imagination in faith, I want you to say something positive about it, as if you are really there in that moment, watching it happen. That's right: I want you to say actual words. (Don't worry about the girl sitting at the coffee shop table next to you. Sure, she might think you're a little crazy, but just hold the book up so she can see the cover; she'll realize you're just full of 𝕮𝖗𝖆𝖟𝖞 𝕱𝖆𝖎𝖙𝖍.) Go ahead and get that image in your mind. Imagine that the multiple obstacles that once stood in the way of this mountain you were facing have all suddenly and miraculously been removed. Take a deep breath and receive that reality. Let it sink in. How do you feel? Say so out loud. Take all the time you need to freely express your gratitude to the God who already made it happen.

Are you back yet? If not, I'll wait. I want you to soak up the full experience of that powerful moment, because it's building momentum for your next step of faith.

For me, this exercise has proven to be so important that (ironically) it's hard for me to put into words. Stating aloud what God is doing and promises to do allows me to see my life and issues from His perspective. It reminds me to praise our omnipotent God in advance for the miracle He has yet to bring to pass and encourages my faith to trust that He actually *will* make it happen for me.

Too many Christians think faith-

> THINKING ABOUT FAITH ISN'T ENOUGH; YOU'VE GOT TO SPEAK THE LANGUAGE OF FAITH.

filled thoughts once in a while but don't put their weight on it by making faith-filled declarations. Thinking about faith isn't enough; you've got to speak the language of faith. Romans 10:9 shows us the three steps to receiving the free gift of salvation Christ sacrificed His life to give us. It's as simple as A-B-C: *accept* Him as Lord over your life, *believe* that He died for your sin and was resurrected, and *confess* that you are a sinner in need of a Savior. The third step is just as essential as the first two, but confession is not something you think; it's something you *say*.

I SAID WHAT I SAID

Let me tell you a story about Jesus speaking that's recorded in the gospel of Mark. One morning, Jesus is walking with His disciples, and He's hungry (11:12). He might even be a little hangry, to be honest, because when they walk by a fig tree with no figs on it, He curses the tree: "May no one ever eat your fruit again!" (verse 14).

Lord, I have been there: belly grumbling, thinking I'm gonna get some Fig Newtons . . . and then there's just a gap in the pantry where the Newtons are supposed to be. It's enough to make a man curse.

Anyway, the disciples hear Jesus tell the tree to shrivel up and die without breaking stride, which is so gangster. The Bible doesn't tell us their reaction, but I imagine they look at each other sideways like, *Dang, that's harsh! And kind of weird. We'd better get the Lord something to eat quick.*

They all go about their day in Jerusalem, and then the next morning they pass by the fig tree again—and now the fruitless tree has withered from bottom to top, roots to branches.

Peter remembers what happened the day before and goes, "Yo, look at this craziness! The fig tree You cursed yesterday is dead today!"

And in my imagination, Jesus gives Peter *that look* and keeps on striding. "I said what I said." Like "Are you *really* surprised, bro? How long have you been with Me—three years now? Surely that's long enough for you to know that I do what I say, and what I say I do."

Hebrews 11:3 says, "By faith," (How? *By faith!*), "we understand that the entire universe was formed at God's command." The Father did not think the world into existence. The Son did not think that fruitless fig tree into death. The Holy Spirit does not think believers into confident assurance (Hebrews 10:15).

Jesus's disciples heard Him say, "May no one ever eat your fruit again," so it should come as no surprise twenty-four hours later when they see a withered, lifeless fig tree. A dead tree should be the least surprising thing they see all day.

Jesus said what He said. And that's how He does it.

You may have heard a different crazy story before: the story of Eve's encounter with a talking serpent in the Garden of Eden. (That's right, I said there was a snake that talked. Back in the early days of Genesis, it apparently wasn't that crazy for animals to talk to humans.) One sunny afternoon, Eve is out picking fruit, gathering groceries for dinner. She wanders into the center of the garden where she and her husband live, where God provides everything they need. And there it is, standing tall with shiny green leaves on strong branches full of the ripest, juiciest-looking fruit

> "I DO WHAT I SAY, AND WHAT I SAY I DO."

she's ever seen: the tree of the knowledge of good and evil. She knows this is the tree God has commanded her and Adam not to eat from—but it looks *sooooo* good. She'll just stand here and admire it for a minute.

Just then, a serpent crawls over and begins saying tricky things that make her doubt God. "Did God *really* say you can't eat *any* of the fruit in the garden?" he coaxes, in what must be a creepy, slimy, slithering, suggestive voice. Eve knows good and well God has prohibited her and Adam only from eating the fruit of that *one* tree, but the serpent is a cunning manipulator. He wants to convince her to lose faith in the Father. "He knows that if you eat this fruit, your eyes will be opened and you'll be like Him . . . and He doesn't want that." *All lies!* But still, it's enough for Eve to lose faith, pick a piece of fruit from that forbidden tree, and bite into it—and then offer some to her husband.

You can read the full story in Genesis 3. It goes on to report that, in response, God evicts Eve and Adam from the garden He had made especially for them. He has to make them leave their paradise the same way He previously had to banish Lucifer (who went on to become the satanic serpent in Eve's story) out of heaven. Later, Jesus would say the devil's native tongue is lies (John 8:44). He is the father of lies. He revels in deceptive manipulation that misleads the people of God into sin.

I want to point out something you may not have noticed. All the Enemy can do is *make suggestions*. Even when that serpent was able to speak out loud, all he could do was make twisted implications in an attempt to get Eve to second-guess what she knew by faith.

The Enemy messes with our minds to influence our real-world actions against God's will. It's up to us to believe his lies and act on them or believe God's truth and act in faith. When we speak godly confessions from our mouths, we interrupt the suggestions of the Enemy in our minds. When we have the truth of God's Word hidden in our hearts, the Enemy can come at us with a whole arsenal of slimy suggestions, but we know to declare, "That's not what God said!"

Not today, Satan!

That's exactly what Jesus does when that ol' snake comes to Him in the desert and starts hissing distorted proposals (Matthew 4:1–11). Jesus has been fasting alone in the wilderness for forty days and nights. Matthew's gospel tells us He "became very hungry" (verse 2). (You think?) So He's hungry and, I imagine, pretty lonely by now—and that's when the devil shows up to spit some lies.

Three times the Enemy offers Jesus a twisted, deceptive version of what the Father intends to accomplish through the Son on the earth. And three times Jesus answers him, "The Scriptures say . . ."

"The Scriptures say . . ."

"The Scriptures say . . ."

Finally, verse 11 says, "The devil went away." Why?

Because Jesus speaks the truth in response to the Evil One's lies and the Enemy can't do a thing about it.

He said what He said. *Boom.*

Now, when I say you need to speak the truth, I mean you need to speak *God's* truth: *God's* desires, *God's* principles, *God's* plans. There is no other truth.

> **STOP HOLDING BACK STATEMENTS OF FAITH IN AN ATTEMPT TO PROTECT GOD'S REPUTATION IN CASE IT DOESN'T HAPPEN.**

I have people ask me often, "What if I say it and it doesn't happen? What if I put my **Crazy Faith** out there and I look stupid?" My question to you is "What do you have to lose?" Stop holding back statements of faith in an attempt to protect God's reputation in case it doesn't happen. God has never needed you to defend Him. If He says something, He's going to do it. His promises don't return void.

> So shall My word be that goes forth from My mouth;
> It shall not return to Me void,
> But it shall accomplish what I please,
> And it shall prosper in the thing for which I sent it.
>   (Isaiah 55:11, NKJV)

We all face difficult circumstances in life, and it can be challenging to speak declarations of faith when all we see around us are facts and devastation that leave us worried and fearful. This is *the* major reason why we hide God's Word in our hearts (a.k.a. read scripture, memorize scripture, and say scripture). Memory verses aren't just for little kids in Sunday school. You need them too! Think about this. If Jesus needed to have the Word ready on demand when the Enemy came to tempt Him, so do we. A good scripture in a bad situation produces faith. When you commit scripture to memory, the Holy Spirit can cause His Word to pop to the front of your mind at the exact moment your faith is most in need. Scripture memorization is like backup files stored in the virtual cloud—just when you thought your local hard drive was fried and you'd lost it all, the cloud backup kicks in to restore everything.

I want to get you started with some faith-filled declarations that come straight out of the Word of God. Please add to this list as you read and study so that your faith continues to strengthen and grow in what God says about you and in His promises to you. Start memorizing now so you can speak truth to the Enemy's lies.

> ## A GOOD SCRIPTURE IN A BAD SITUATION PRODUCES FAITH.

STATING FAITH SCRIPTURES

Don't worry about anything; instead, pray about everything. Tell God what you need, and thank him for all he has done. Then you will experience God's peace, which exceeds anything we can understand. His peace will guard your hearts and minds as you live in Christ Jesus. (Philippians 4:6–7)

I have hidden your word in my heart,
    that I might not sin against you. (Psalm 119:11)

If anyone is in Christ, the new creation has come: The old has gone, the new is here! (2 Corinthians 5:17, NIV)

It is by grace you have been saved, through faith—and this is not from yourselves, it is the gift of God—not by works, so that no one can boast. (Ephesians 2:8–9, NIV)

Trust in the LORD with all your heart,
And lean not on your own understanding;
In all your ways acknowledge Him,
    and He shall direct your paths. (Proverbs 3:5–6, NKJV)

"I know the plans I have for you," declares the LORD, "plans to prosper you and not to harm you, plans to give you hope and a future." (Jeremiah 29:11, NIV)

As for me and my house, we will serve the LORD. (Joshua 24:15, NKJV)

We know that in all things God works for the good of those who love him, who have been called according to his purpose. (Romans 8:28, NIV)

Come to me, all you who are weary and burdened, and I will give you rest. Take my yoke upon you and learn from me, for I am gentle and humble in heart, and you will find rest for your souls. For my yoke is easy and my burden is light. (Matthew 11:28–30, NIV)

My God will meet all your needs according to the riches of his glory in Christ Jesus. (Philippians 4:19, NIV)

I am convinced that neither death nor life, neither angels nor demons, neither the present nor the future, nor any powers, neither height nor depth, nor anything else in all creation, will be able to separate us from the love of God that is in Christ Jesus our Lord. (Romans 8:38–39, NIV)

Have I not commanded you? Be strong and courageous. Do not be afraid; do not be discouraged, for the LORD your God will be with you wherever you go. (Joshua 1:9, NIV)

The LORD is my light and my salvation—
whom shall I fear?
The LORD is the stronghold of my life—
of whom shall I be afraid? (Psalm 27:1, NIV)

Your word is a lamp to guide my feet
and a light for my path. (Psalm 119:105)

The word of God will never fail. (Luke 1:37)

Be still, and know that I am God;
I will be exalted among the nations,
I will be exalted in the earth! (Psalm 46:10, NKJV)

Jesus replied: " 'Love the Lord your God with all your heart and with all your soul and with all your mind.' This is the first and greatest commandment. And the second is like it: 'Love your neighbor as yourself.' " (Matthew 22:37–39, NIV)

Whatever you do, work at it with all your heart, as working for the Lord, not for human masters. (Colossians 3:23, NIV)

The fruit of the Spirit is love, joy, peace, forbearance, kindness, goodness, faithfulness, gentleness and self-control. Against such things there is no law. (Galatians 5:22–23, NIV)

No temptation has overtaken you except what is common to mankind. And God is faithful; he will not let you be tempted beyond what you can bear. But when you are tempted, he will also provide a way out so that you can endure it. (1 Corinthians 10:13, NIV)

For more, check out the Stating Faith Scriptures at the back of this book.

I encourage you to put these scriptures where you can find them: on your refrigerator, mirror, dashboard—maybe even make it your lock screen on your phone. Grab your list of biblical faith declarations, and start stating faith. Out loud. Take action to memorize what God says so that when the Enemy whispers lies, you can move in stating faith.

SAY IT WHEN YOU CAN'T SEE IT

Mark 10 tells the story of a blind man named Bartimaeus. Jesus strolls into Jericho with His disciples, and a large crowd begins to follow them. Sitting on the side of the road is blind Bartimaeus. He hears that Jesus is walking by, and he can't resist. He's heard about this Jesus and how He has healed the lame, cast demons out, restored the sick, and especially how He has made the blind see. Bartimaeus has suffered too long and wants a piece of that healing.

So he starts calling Jesus's name—not just calling but *yelling*. There is passion behind his proclamation. I want you to get this: Bartimaeus cannot see. He's not sure if his yelling is actually getting Jesus's attention. He doesn't know if Jesus is turning around to come to him. He doesn't even know how close or far Jesus is from him. But he doesn't care. He is speaking in faith.

That is stating faith. It's when you want God so bad that you call out for Him, even if you're not sure that He really hears you or sees you. Bartimaeus needs Jesus desperately. He could just wish Jesus would see him by thinking good thoughts, or he could just whisper Jesus's name hoping Jesus will hear him through the crowd. But Bartimaeus isn't going to let shame, fear, or what others think stop him. So, with all the passion he can muster, he yells for Jesus.

In fact, he yells so loud that the people around him tell him to quiet down. (Side note: Make sure the community around you will help you scream instead of telling you to quiet down when you yell for Jesus. Go ahead and take inventory. You're believing in faith for something, but are your besties and homeboys believing with you? Or are they telling you, "It's not that serious. There's no way that can happen. Girl, you need to move on." Think about it. The people around Bartimaeus can see. They can actually help him get to Jesus if they want. But instead, out of their own fears, they try to shut him up! Do you have friends like that? Let me leave that alone before you have to get a new crew . . .)

After the people around Bartimaeus try to muzzle him, the story tells us that he gets louder with even more zeal. He ignores the crowd and gets what I call ignant (ignorant, for y'all scholars out there). Bartimaeus gets undignified, rowdy, wild. Some may even say . . . crazy. He knows that his situation looks impossible, but if he can only get the attention of Jesus, that could change everything.

> **MAKE SURE THE COMMUNITY AROUND YOU WILL HELP YOU SCREAM INSTEAD OF TELLING YOU TO QUIET DOWN WHEN YOU YELL FOR JESUS.**

When is the last time you got crazy enough to call God into a situation that looked impossible? When is the last time you opened up your mouth and shouted, "Jesus! I need You! Help! See me! Answer me! Come to me!" Bartimaeus knows this is what it's going to take, but some of us are too dignified and proper to do that. Let me encourage you that God says He will make the foolish things confound the wise (1 Corinthians 1:27). You may seem foolish to someone else, but yell louder! Call out to Jesus with enthusiasm, excitement, desperation, and intensity.

> NO MATTER WHAT'S GOING ON ALL AROUND, WHEN YOU CALL OUT TO HIM, YOU, TOO, HAVE JESUS'S FULL ATTENTION.

Jesus hears Bartimaeus and asks for the people to bring the blind man to Him. They tell Bartimaeus that Jesus has called for him. He throws aside his coat, jumps up, and comes to Jesus. And now here he is, standing before the Savior of the world. He can't see Jesus, but Jesus sure can see him. Even though crowds surround him, Bartimaeus has Jesus's full attention. (This should be an encouragement to you. No matter what's going on all around, when you call out to Him, you, too, have Jesus's full attention.)

Jesus asks him, "What do you want me to do for you?" (Mark 10:51). Now, of all the questions Jesus could ask this blind man, why would He ask that? There's no way Jesus doesn't already know that Bartimaeus is blind. I mean, someone probably has to guide him to Jesus. Also, Jesus is God in the flesh.

Don't miss this. Jesus knows what Bartimaeus wants, but

He wants Bartimaeus to say it out loud. He wants Bart to state his faith. Can you place yourself into this story? Look at your situation. Imagine Jesus standing in front of you, looking intently into your eyes, and asking you the same question.

"What do you want Me to do for you?"

You got it in your mind? Do you see what you want Jesus to do for you? How can He heal you, redeem you, set you free? Do you see your lifeless business thriving? The marriage you need Him to mend? The child you want to deliver in health? The job you want? The love you desire? What do you want Jesus to do for you?

In front of the entire crowd, Bart states what he wants *even though he can't see it.* The power of this story is that Bartimaeus *says* what he has not *seen*—literally. He says, "My Rabbi, I want to see!" (verse 51). Look at the exclamation point. Bart doesn't call for Jesus with passion only when he is far off, then get in front of Him and whisper what he wants. He says it with all his might. He says it *loud.* He says it proud. He says it with faith. He says it with his chest! (Google Kevin Hart "with his chest" for reference and a laugh.)

Don't just think it. Don't just wish it. Don't just journal it. Don't mumble it or whisper it. Say it. Yell it. Shout it.

State your faith.

10

FADING FAITH

THE ONE

As a pastor, I'm doing only part of my job if I focus only on people who are in a hopeful season of their lives, who feel ready, inspired, and compelled to take their next step (or steps!) into deeper, more radical 𝕮𝖗𝖆𝖟𝖞 𝕱𝖆𝖎𝖙𝖍. Don't get me wrong. I *love* that part of my job. By nature, I'm loud and rambunctious and enthusiastic and wild, and it's pure joy to let God use the person He created me to be to love and grow and cheer on His people.

But that's not the whole job. *Pastor* in Greek (the original language of the New Testament) means "shepherd,"* and an important part of a shepherd's job is to care for lost, injured, scared, or trapped sheep. In fact, Jesus tells His disciples that good shepherds prioritize lost lambs over sheep that are doing just fine:

If a man has a hundred sheep and one of them wanders away, what will he do? Won't he leave the ninety-nine oth-

---

* Blue Letter Bible, s.v. *"poimēn,"* www.blueletterbible.org/lang/lexicon/lexicon.cfm?Strongs=G4166&t=KJV.

ers on the hills and go out to search for the one that is lost? And if he finds it, I tell you the truth, he will rejoice over it more than over the ninety-nine that didn't wander away! In the same way, it is not my heavenly Father's will that even one of these little ones should perish. (Matthew 18:12–14)

So this chapter is for you if you're "the one" whose faith is fading. (And if that's not you right now, it will be at some point. Life is *real*.)

Here's the truth: I've been "the one" off and on the past five years, the one with *fading* faith. Not in every area of my life—the incredible transformation of Transforma-

> ## GOOD SHEPHERDS PRIORITIZE LOST LAMBS OVER SHEEP THAT ARE DOING JUST FINE.

tion Church has unfolded during the same time period, and my **Crazy Faith** for what God will do for, in, and through our community hasn't wavered since that 2015 morning in Isabella's room. But ministry isn't the only area of life that requires faith for our family.

I told you in the last chapter about my little hero, MJ, diagnosed with autism a few years ago. And the truth is, I have had some dark days since then. Let me get even more H.O.T. (humble, open, and transparent) with you: I still do.

LOSS IS REAL

Everybody experiences loss. No one is exempt. Yes, we are God's worthy, beloved children who are heirs with Christ of

God's glory—but we reside in a world that is broken. I'm so thankful Jesus came to be with us in this brokenness and make everything new through the power of His resurrection! But often He does that re-creating *in* and *through*, not *out of*. He doesn't always take us out of pain and loss—but He always, *always* redeems and restores our pain and loss to His glory and ours. The apostle Paul tells the Christians in Rome, who are experiencing intense persecution from the government,

> Since we are his children, we are his heirs. In fact, together with Christ we are heirs of God's glory. But if we are to share his glory, we must also share his suffering. (Romans 8:17)

When we are in Christ, He brings new life *in* and *through* the hardships and disappointments we suffer in this broken world.

I have to remind myself of this rock-solid resurrection promise almost every time I drive MJ to therapy. Some days I have **Crazy Faith** for what God will do in and through His precious child MJ's life and in and through our family's life with our little hero. But other days my faith starts to fade. Stating aloud our God's promises for MJ as we drive to speech therapy sometimes feels like the hardest thing I ever do. And honestly, if MJ doesn't make significant progress in his appointment that day, then it feels even harder to speak God's truth over him next time.

Maybe you lived in purity, married a God-seeking spouse, prayed together for your future kids, and trusted God for the blessing of children. But now, years later, you've tried every fertility treatment available with no result, and your faith is fading.

Maybe you started that business and did everything right—practiced integrity, acted with generosity to employees and customers, gave 10 percent of your profits to kingdom causes—but then the pandemic hit and shut you down, and your faith is fading.

Maybe you and your siblings were raised in a loving home with both parents pushing you toward your dreams, calling, and purpose. You always talked about how amazing they'd be as grandparents—only to get an unexpected call that their car crashed and their lives were abruptly ended. Now you're forced to live without them, and your faith is fading.

Maybe you were a young, healthy, active person who prided yourself on athleticism and fitness. Out of the blue, you started to feel like your body was breaking down and suffered a stroke. You survived, but now you have the daunting task of relearning how to talk, walk, and function as normal, and your faith is fading.

Maybe you have been married for twenty-two years, raised kids, and built a home with the love of your life. The emotional distance has been evident for a while, but you never thought it would end in infidelity. You're committed to stay and work it out, but your spouse refuses and decides that divorce is the best option; he wants to start a new life with someone else. The devastation is paralyzing, and your faith is fading.

Maybe you excelled in high school, made straight As, tested high, and graduated with all types of honors. You got accepted into your dream college and found out that scholarships wouldn't cover tuition. The thought of going to your local community college makes you feel like a failure, and your faith is fading.

> ## PROFOUND LOSS CAN CAUSE CRAZY FAITH TO FADE.

Maybe you inherited a home that has been in your family for years, full of memories, moments, and milestones. But a violent tornado ripped through your county, causing catastrophic damage to the whole region—including your family's beloved estate. You're collecting the remnants of what used to be your life, and your faith is fading.

Maybe you are watching the news and hear that another unarmed Black man has been gunned down at the hands of police. As much as you enjoy the freedoms of our country, you are once again reminded that you have two Black sons, a nephew, and a Black brother in a world that doesn't view them as equal. You're trying to hold on to hope, but your faith is fading.

Maybe you have faithfully followed your mentor and spiritual leader since adolescence, and the person you are today is a direct result of the lessons, leadership, and lifestyle she modeled for you. Rumors of moral failure start to circulate and eventually are publicly confirmed. The person you thought you knew has been living a double life, and your faith is fading.

Profound loss can cause **Crazy Faith** to fade.

Everybody—every human being on the planet—experiences loss. Not in the same way, not at the same time. But loss comes to the doorstep of every one of us who live in this fallen world, whether or not we are seeking God. What in the world are we supposed to do with that? How do unexpected loss and **Crazy Faith** go together?

If you're in a season of failure, heartbreak, or discouragement, I have good news—for you and me both. Not shout-

and-clap, live-in-denial, optimistic-meme news, but the real thing. Actually *good* good news.

UNTIL I SEE IT

If you feel like you've missed out on significant, life-changing opportunities, just imagine how Thomas is feeling when all the other disciples tell him they've seen the risen Lord. Jesus had appeared among them, breathed on them, and imparted the Holy Spirit—only Thomas wasn't there when it happened. Talk about feeling like you missed out.

Check out his response when they give him the news:

One of the twelve disciples, Thomas (nicknamed the Twin), was not with the others when Jesus came. They told him, "We have seen the Lord!" But he replied, "I won't believe it unless I see the nail wounds in his hands, put my fingers into them, and place my hand into the wound in his side." (John 20:24–25)

All the other disciples have this 𝕮𝖗𝖆𝖟𝖞 𝕱𝖆𝖎𝖙𝖍 encounter with the Leader they thought was dead and gone. They're grieving. They're feeling His loss down deep, disillusioned about all they've sacrificed to follow someone they believed in, terrified for their lives and futures. And suddenly, here He is! Standing among them, speaking peace to them, showing them the scars that are evidence of His resurrection. John tells us, "They were filled with joy when they saw the Lord!" (verse 20).

You think?

Jesus shows up for them. He comes to meet them in the

moment of their deepest loss and—just like you or I would be—the disciples are *hyped*.

But when Jesus shows up, Thomas isn't there.

Now, I want to make something clear: the Bible doesn't tell us why. John doesn't say, "Thomas wasn't there because he was out sinning like crazy" or "Thomas cursed God and ran away." Tom might be out running errands. He might be the only disciple who's not too scared to go out and get food for everybody. In fact, I think this is a pretty likely explanation. Remember the story we looked at in the last chapter about Martha? When Jesus tells the disciples it's time to get over to Bethany to see about "waking" Lazarus from sleep, some of them are nervous because a couple weeks ago when they were there, the neighbors tried to kill Jesus. *Does it really seem like a good idea to go back, Lord?*

Look what Thomas says: "Let's go, too—and die with Jesus" (John 11:16). That is a legit action hero line right there—so it's easy for me to believe that after Jesus's death, Thomas, a.k.a. Dwayne "The Rock" Johnson, is the one disciple with enough guts to take care of the other panicked guys. Either way, the Bible doesn't say why Tom isn't with the other disciples. It may not be his fault.

Your loss may not be your fault. Sometimes it's just . . . life.

> **YOUR LOSS MAY NOT BE YOUR FAULT. SOMETIMES IT'S JUST . . . LIFE.**

Ever wonder why you were born into an abusive home? Why you saw those disturbing images at such a young age? Why you didn't get picked? Why you were bullied? Why you lost a child? Why you were diagnosed with cancer? Why you had to file for bankruptcy? Why your home was robbed? Why you had the accident? Why you're still not married?

I sincerely wish I had answers for you.

He gives his sunlight to both the evil and the good, and he sends rain on the just and the unjust alike. (Matthew 5:45)

If part of you feels like all the bad things that have ever happened to you are somehow your fault, I want to free you from the bondage of that lie. Sometimes it's just life. It's not fair. Thomas didn't necessarily do anything to deserve being late to the resurrected Lord's appearance, and neither did you deserve to suffer the consequences of other people's choices.

And just like Tom isn't hyped with **Crazy Faith** when the rest of the crew experiences a miracle, it's okay if you're not hyped. Thomas is like, "Yo, that's fine and good for y'all, but this miracle you're saying you experienced does nothing for me. Maybe shut up about it, 'cause y'all on my nerves. Until *I* get a miracle, you can miss me with all this **Crazy Faith** nonsense."

I want you to know that I've been in that moment more than once. It's the "God, if You don't show me *something* . . ." moment, when it feels impossible, even unimaginable, to believe without seeing.

HOPING TO SEE

Fading faith starts with **Crazy Faith**. It's desolation that settles deep in our bones *after* we've experienced what God can do but then we don't see the miracle we're hoping for when we need it. I want to remind you that Thomas walked with Jesus. He wasn't some oblivious unbeliever; he knew firsthand through his own direct, eyewitness experience what Jesus could do. But then Tom lost Him—and when you know personally what Jesus can do and then you take a big loss, Crazy Faith can turn to fading faith real quick.

Faith can fade when you only hear about what you hope to see.

Tom hears about a miracle that all the other disciples got to experience for themselves. And let's be real, it's a miracle he desperately hopes to see too. That's why I have such a problem with the nickname Doubting Thomas. It's not like Tom is some kind of skeptical atheist crusader who has already decided that there's no such thing as miracles. He's not Doubting Thomas. He's Hurting Thomas. He's Brokenhearted Thomas. He's Exhausted Thomas.

> FAITH CAN FADE WHEN YOU ONLY HEAR ABOUT WHAT YOU HOPE TO SEE.

On those drives to therapy with MJ, I'm not Doubting Michael. I'm Tired Michael, devoted follower of Jesus and loving father to MJ, who is hurting and sad for my boy, has seen time after time what God can do, and is desperate for Him to show up again.

We don't live on the mountaintop all the time. Valleys are part of our landscape as believers too. Marriages go through hell. Parents die. Kids break our hearts. Viruses spread out of control. Markets fall and fail. Tornadoes and earthquakes and hurricanes strike.

When you walk through your valley, when real life happens, I'm asking you to take a note from our boy Hopeful Thomas.

Eight days later the disciples were together again, and this time Thomas was with them. The doors were locked; but suddenly, as before, Jesus was standing among them. "Peace be with you," he said. Then he said to Thomas, "Put your finger here, and look at my hands. Put your hand into the wound in my side. Don't be faithless any longer. Believe!"

"My Lord and my God!" Thomas exclaimed. (John 20:26–28)

Notice anything? *This time Thomas is with them.* He still hasn't gotten the miracle he's been hoping for, but you cannot get rid of this dude. He just keeps showing up. He's probably sick to death of hearing his bros blabbing about what they've seen and experienced—but here's Tom, still showing up. And notice, too, that the other disciples are all good with him being there. They haven't kicked him out of the club because his faith is fading. He's one of them. Even in the fading, Tom belongs.

> WE DON'T LIVE ON THE MOUNTAINTOP ALL THE TIME. VALLEYS ARE PART OF OUR LANDSCAPE AS BELIEVERS TOO.

My hurting, brokenhearted, exhausted friend: you belong. Your fading faith can't exclude you from God's family any more than bad breath can. (Do us a favor and brush your teeth, though.) It may be painful to stick around when it seems like everybody else is getting the miracle you're hoping for, but hear me when I say: among His people is where Jesus is most likely to show up. He can show up anywhere; that's one of the perks of being God. But when you get some Jesus seekers to-

> **AMONG HIS PEOPLE IS WHERE JESUS IS MOST LIKELY TO SHOW UP.**

gether, calling on heaven's store-house of blessing to be poured out on hurting people who are hoping against hope to see a miracle—well, that's just math. (Nah, I'm playing. It's Jesus's own promise: "Where two or three gather to-gether as my followers, I am there among them," Matthew 18:20.)

Thomas sticks around—and Jesus shows up. He hits a rerun of eight days ago, appearing out of nowhere in the locked room where the disciples are laying low. Notice some-thing else: Jesus doesn't waste time chatting up the guys who got their miracle last week, those who are already hyped with 𝕮𝖗𝖆𝖟𝖞 𝕱𝖆𝖎𝖙𝖍. He speaks peace to the whole room and then turns directly to Hopeful Thomas, who doesn't even have to explain himself. The risen Lord already knows Thomas's needs, and He has shown up tonight to bring what Tom has been hoping for: Himself.

SEEING CRAZY GRACE

Don't miss this. Jesus meets Tom's need for physical confir-mation of His resurrection—but He does so in order for Thomas *to believe*. Not so Tom can brag around town that he got to touch the Lord and other people didn't, *nyah-nyah*. Not so Tom can get a book contract or sell his story to *People* magazine or get more Instagram sponsors. Not even so Thomas won't be the only, lonely member of the Disciples Who Didn't See Jesus Club.

No, the point is for Thomas to trust again. To believe. To

regain the confidence he had before Jesus was crucified, in a hundredfold measure. Fading faith attracts God's crazy grace. Our God is not dismayed or repelled by your loss, failure, or disappointment, just as He was not dismayed or repelled by Thomas's doubt. Instead, God responds with crazy grace in three ways to His well-beloved kids whose faith is fading:

1. He meets a *tangible* need.
2. He meets a *visual* need.
3. He meets a *personal* need.

Jesus invites Thomas to touch Him, to see Him, and to know Him personally—and that's why Tom believes. Not because he hears a prophetic word from one of the other disciples but because Jesus acts tangibly, visually, and personally for him.

Thomas tells his bros what he's hoping for—"I [hope to] see the nail wounds in his hands, put my fingers into them, and place my hand into the wound in his side"— and that's an important step for us too. So many times, God shows us His crazy grace tangibly, visually, and personally *through His people*. Yes, He *can* meet the needs you express to Him in secret. But that's not how He designed the church to work. The apostle Paul writes to the Galatian Christians:

> **FADING FAITH ATTRACTS GOD'S CRAZY GRACE.**

Share each other's burdens, and in this way obey the law of Christ. If you think you are too important to help someone, you are only fooling yourself. You are not that important. (Galatians 6:2–3)

Paul's not giving the Galatians some sass. He's giving them the secret to following Christ's way of life. Some people's burdens are just too heavy to carry alone, and Christians who want to follow Christ will generously and joyfully take some of that weight. This means that those with heavy burdens *must be willing to share.*

I'm so deeply thankful for my community and my church family who have chosen to lovingly share Natalie's and my burden in all that comes with raising a son with special needs. From friends who have allowed us to stay in their home during a dark season of depression; to family members who gather in prayer for us weekly; to people who send articles, emails, and videos of encouragement to spark our 𝔠𝔯𝔞𝔷𝔶 𝔣𝔞𝔦𝔱𝔥—each of these acts of grace is tangible, visible, and personal.

God doesn't provide just saving grace. God also provides *sustaining* grace. At the time I write this book, we are still in the middle of believing for a miracle. But even if God doesn't change MJ's situation, we know that He *will* sustain us through it.

When we got the call confirming that MJ has autism, I went to the place that makes me feel safe♪music. With tears in my eyes, I began to pen these words:

You sustain
You sustain
In the middle of it all
You remain the same
Through the rain
You still reign
You sustain

Your promises always come true
Not depending on me but relying on You
Your mercies are new every day
So I will trust You

These words have been an anchor for me, and I pray they'll be an anchor for you. No matter what you've been through. No matter what has happened. No matter how you feel right now. I'm a living witness that God *will* sustain you in your season of fading faith. I believe He's preparing you for a season of even CRAZIER FAITH yet to come.

11

SAVING FAITH

CHRISTMAS IN JULY (OR WHENEVER)

Has it ever occurred to you that the events leading up to Jesus's birth didn't happen at Christmastime? It's pretty obvious once you think about it—Christmas didn't exist yet!—but sometimes we get hung up on talking about the birth of Jesus only during the month of December. But from Mary and Joseph's point of view, all the craziness unfolding in their lives happened on a regular Tuesday (or whenever). And since God shows up in *our* lives on regular Tuesdays (or whenever), Jesus's earthly parents-to-be are awesome models for how to live in 𝕮𝖗𝖆𝖟𝖞 𝕱𝖆𝖎𝖙𝖍. So, whether you're reading this on Christmas or the Fourth of July or Father's Day or any day ending in *y*, get in the Christmas spirit with me for the next few minutes.

When we're H.O.T. (humble, open, and transparent) with one another, we admit life is crazy. Our families are crazy. Our jobs are crazy. Politics is crazy. And here's the thing: it's the same for Joseph and Mary. Their homeland is ruled by the foreign military superpower of that time, the Roman Empire, and the Romans have no time or patience for Jewish worship, customs, beliefs, and traditions. They want the Jews to get with the pagan program and stop acting like they are God's special chosen people. There is religious and cultural persecution, massive inequality, and political unrest all around. (Does any of this sound familiar?) Anyway, life is already crazy—and that's exactly when God shows up.

> # LIFE IS ALREADY CRAZY—AND THAT'S EXACTLY WHEN GOD SHOWS UP.

Mary is engaged to marry Joseph, but before their wedding, the gospel of Matthew tells us, "she became pregnant through the power of the Holy Spirit. Joseph, to whom she was engaged, was a righteous man and did not want to disgrace her publicly, so he decided to break the engagement quietly" (1:18–19).

As if life isn't crazy enough, the Holy Spirit comes to disrupt all their plans.

In my holy imagination, Mary breaks the news to her fiancé and then Joseph goes for a long, angry, frustrated walk, muttering to himself the whole way. "Why she got to mess it all up? We made promises. We had dreams! We were gonna travel and have adventures before settling down to have Joe Jr. and his little brothers and sisters. And now Mary done messed it up." Joseph gets so agitated and bent out of shape in his emotions that he does what most of us do when our feelings get to be too much: he takes a nap. But then

> an angel of the Lord appeared to him in a dream. "Joseph, son of David," the angel said, "do not be afraid to take Mary as your wife. For the child within her was conceived by the Holy Spirit. And she will have a son, and you are to

name him Jesus, for he will save his people from their sins."
(verses 20–21)

Now, if I were Joseph, I'd be like, "Be straight with me: life
is already crazy, I'm already in this entirely jacked-up situation, and now You're giving me *instructions and responsibilities?*"

Let me be straight with you: yep.

CRAZY WORD

I know for a fact that you've never been in Joseph's exact
situation, but I'm willing to bet you've felt the same way in
your own set of crazy circumstances. I know I have. *Really?
Right now? On top of everything else that's going on, now
God's asking me to do something* extra *crazy?*

This is how God does, time and time and time again. Why?
Because our God loves to use crazy things that don't make
sense to sensible people to confound anybody who thinks he's
got it all figured out. Check this:

> God chose things the world considers foolish in order to
> shame those who think they are wise. And he chose things
> that are powerless to shame those who are powerful. God
> chose things despised by the world, things counted as noth-
> ing at all, and used them to bring to nothing what the
> world considers important. As a result, no one can ever
> boast in the presence of God. (1 Corinthians 1:27–29)

God chose Joseph and Mary to play essential roles in His
rescue operation for humanity for the same reason He chose

a twenty-something Black man with a mug shot and six months of community college to grow a local church and start a worldwide movement. Not making sense is our God's MO, because if it made sense, we could take the credit. (Take note: His plans *always* make sense on the back end, when we're through to the other side, but at the beginning? Straight-up crazy.)

God gets the ball rolling for our journey of 𝕮𝖗𝖆𝖟𝖞 𝕱𝖆𝖎𝖙𝖍 by first giving a *crazy word*. It might come in a dream (like for Joseph), during early morning prayer in your daughter's bedroom (like for me), or from a friend who texts you out of the blue because you've been on his mind. It could come from a preacher on Sunday morning, a book you read before bed on Wednesday, or a TikTok you watch

> **NOT MAKING SENSE IS OUR GOD'S MO, BECAUSE IF IT MADE SENSE, WE COULD TAKE THE CREDIT.**

waiting for your Friday afternoon teeth cleaning. However it comes, it won't make sense to anybody else. (For that matter, it might not make sense to *you*.)

God's crazy word often comes in the darkest of times. We already talked about the dark and crazy times Joseph and Mary were living through, but your crazy word from God will also come in darkness. And that's a good thing, because Psalm 119 says, "Your word is a lamp to guide my feet and a light for my path" (verse 105). When God's crazy word comes, it gives just enough light for you to take the next step, then the next, and then the next. You obey. You forgive. You meet with Him in prayer. You take a risk. You wait on Him and serve His people.

When His crazy word comes, don't get paralyzed trying to please other people. Of course we would all like everyone to agree with God's crazy word to us, but His timing for them isn't necessarily His timing for you. It would be convenient and comforting for Mary if an angel appeared to her and Joseph at the same time. But the fact that God waits to give a crazy word to Joseph doesn't make His crazy word to her any less true, timely, or powerful.

CRAZY WORRY

Once you get a crazy word, it's only a matter of time before the Enemy attacks with crazy worry. As we've seen, all he can do is make suggestions—but when those sneaky whispers come into darkness so thick you can't see two steps ahead, they can be so hard to ignore.

About a minute and a half after I finished writing down the vision of Transformation Church moving into the SpiritBank Event Center, all the *how* questions flooded my mind. *God, how in the world are You gonna take a crazy Black dude born in South Tulsa, move him to North Tulsa to take over a church from a white man, let me be myself, and build a multiethnic, multigenerational, multiplying, and multicampus church? For that matter, how in the world are You going to touch the whole world through our little North Tulsa ministry? How? How?*

For a minute there, I got stuck in the *how* and forgot about the *who*.

This reminds me of one time I went to a super-bougie restaurant for dinner at the invitation of a multimillionaire. It was so bougie, there were no prices on the menu. Now, for someone who's used to feeding the whole family at Cheddar's for $32.99, the lack of prices was anxiety inducing. "Order anything you want," is what my host said, but all I could think about was not being greedy or offending him. So we're sitting there while the server awkwardly waits on me to order, and my host goes, "What's the problem?"

"Uhhhh . . . I can't decide between the filet mignon and the duck."

He looks at the server and says, "He'll have both."

And I'm like, "Hold on, hold on! I'm not hungry enough to eat them both."

He shrugs. "So you'll take the extra to go. Don't worry so much."

That has stuck with me and become a mantra as I step out in 𝕮𝖗𝖆𝖟𝖞 𝕱𝖆𝖎𝖙𝖍 again and again. And now I'm passing it on to you: "Don't worry so much." You are hereby authorized not to worry. God knows exactly what He's

> **WORRY ADDS NOTHING BUT TAKES EVERYTHING.**

doing. He has more than enough to pay the bill. As a matter of fact, it's already paid!

My friend, God is more interested in providing for your purpose and destiny than that rich dude was for duck and filet mignon. You might be worried about the how, but He ain't worried one little bit.

Paul wrote to the Philippian Christians some straightforward advice for times when they got anxious: "Don't worry." (It doesn't get any more straightforward than that!)

Don't worry about anything; instead, pray about everything. Tell God what you need, and thank him for all he has done. Then you will experience God's peace, which exceeds anything we can understand. His peace will guard your hearts and minds as you live in Christ Jesus. (Philippians 4:6–7)

Pray about what? *Everything.* The job I should take? *Everything.* The person I should marry? *Everything.* Where to go on vacation? *Everything.* You may not get the car or the house at exactly the moment you want it, but you *will* experience God's peace that passes all understanding. And let me tell you from experience: worry adds nothing but takes everything—except the peace that only God can give. He's big enough to handle the how.

CRAZY WALK

You got a crazy word, you're letting God deal with the crazy worry in prayer, and now it's time to walk the crazy walk. We've talked time and again in this book about the daily discipline of faith, about turning lazy faith into active faith, about doing our own prophetic work, about faith expressing itself as love through good works. At some point, we just have to decide and then get walking.

Mary and Joseph get their crazy word, and you know they must have some crazy worry, but if they are going to make it from their hometown of Nazareth to Bethlehem, Jesus's prophesied birthplace, they have to start walking. Those ninety miles can't walk themselves.

> IF YOU CAN SEE IT, YOU DON'T NEED FAITH.

As crazy as it sounds, have you started walking? If you're waiting to see the whole trip in advance, receive this word from 2 Corinthians 5:7: "We walk by faith, not by sight" (NKJV). This scripture always takes me back to the '90s TGIF lineup on ABC. Between Urkel asking, "Did I do that?" and my junior-high relationship goal, Topanga on *Boy Meets World*, y'all remember *Step by Step*? The theme song said, "Step by step, day by day"—and that's exactly how we walk the crazy walk of faith. Step by step. One foot in front of the other. Day by day, in daily faith.

If you can see it, you don't need faith. If you *can't* see it, though—faith is a requirement. Even if it means you have to take baby steps, it's time to get walking.

CRAZY WAIT

Joseph and his bride don't take one step and then instantly arrive in Bethlehem. Ninety miles is a long walk, y'all. That's South Tulsa to Oklahoma City, Dallas to Waco, Chicago to South Bend, Manhattan to Philadelphia, San Francisco to Modesto. And we're not talking about firing up the Escalade and hopping on the interstate. We're taking one dusty step at a time through dry, rocky wilderness with a very pregnant lady. (And I know personally from walking with my wife through four pregnancies, including swollen ankles, shortness of breath, and frequent potty breaks, nobody's getting to Bethlehem quick.)

Once you get the faith to start walking out God's crazy word, it may take a minute to get there. And let's be honest: waiting sucks. But remember "Waiting Faith"? Waiting doesn't mean sitting around scrolling Twitter or bingeing HBO. Waiting means service. Get used to saying, "How can I help? Do you need anything else? It would be my pleasure." Waiting always means serving others. Don't waste your wait.

The waiting is where God makes you into who you need to be when He gets you there. For your marriage to be healed and whole, you may have to go to counseling. For you to be an effective CEO of that future company, you may have to read some books, take some classes, and get a mentor. For you to minister with integrity and power to millions, you will have to develop character and wisdom in private with Him. For you to win back your wounded child's trust, you will have to prove your trustworthiness with patience, endurance, and grace.

Paul says in his letter to the Galatians,

> Let's not get tired of doing what is good. At just the right time we will reap a harvest of blessing if we don't give up. (6:9)

Those last five words are the key to the whole thing: *if we don't give up.* That's a big if, but I promise the payoff, which will come "at just the right time," will be worth the crazy wait. Ask me on date night, when I have to wait for Natalie to finish what she calls her "process." Sometimes I despair of ever getting a bite to eat, but then she comes down the hall looking like a supermodel. Worth it. *So* worth it.

The right time is coming. I believe it for you. I believe it for your family. I believe it for your business. I believe it for your spiritual, physical, mental, emotional, and financial health.

Don't give up.

CRAZY WAY

This is my favorite part: when God makes a crazy way. My God specializes in parting Red Seas, in knocking down walls, in multiplying oil enough for the whole neighborhood, in giving paralyzed people power to walk home, in taking a wet and wavy stroll with a hyped disciple, in making a way where there is no way.

But sometimes the crazy way He makes looks nothing like we expect.

Think about Mary and Joseph again. If we didn't already know their story, we would expect a fairy-tale ending once they arrive in Bethlehem. Surely when they get there, the mayor or a rich wine merchant will roll out the red carpet and throw them a parade and then put them up in the honeymoon suite at the Four Seasons Hotel! But what happens instead? "There was no room for them in the inn" (Luke 2:7, NKJV).

You may be too young to remember this, but back in the day before smartphones and digital cameras, we took pictures on physical film that then had to be developed through a special process in a darkroom. If film was exposed to light before it was fully developed in darkness, it would be ruined.

The crazy way God makes for the mother and stepfather of His beloved Son is in the darkroom, in an obscure and out-of-the-way place where His plan for the world could fully develop. Let that be an encouragement to you: in the darkness and obscurity you're waiting in right now, He is developing His image in you.

Joseph and Mary's darkroom is a stable where farm animals that aren't housebroken are put up for the night. Imag-

> IN THE DARKNESS AND OBSCURITY YOU'RE WAITING IN RIGHT NOW, HE IS DEVELOPING HIS IMAGE IN YOU.

ine how much crap there is just lying around! I'm sure God had a million reasons for not choosing the Ritz-Carlton of Bethlehem, but I'm also convinced that one was to show us His favorite crazy way to bring new life: out of the crap.

Out of the crap, God brought new life to the whole world.

Out of the crap, God will bring new life to, in, and through you.

Out of the crap your family has been dealing with, out of the crap your business has faced, out of the crap news you just got at the doctor's office, out of your crap childhood—new life is taking root, and *at just the right time,* it will bloom into the light. If Christ was born into a crappy situation (pun intended), just imagine what God can do with your crappy situation.

This is God's crazy way.

More times than I can count, I have gotten myself into crappy situations. Sometimes it has felt to me like there was no coming back into the light. I almost believed the lie that God was appalled and repelled by the stink of my actions. I hoped there was a better way. And eventually, thankfully, I found out that there is.

Jesus said, "I am the way, the truth, and the life. No one can come to the Father except through me" (John 14:6). I was going one way, a way that would end in more and more crap, but then I found out there is another Way. His name is Jesus. If you are in a crappy situation like I was, you don't have to keep heading in the same direction. You can get on the Way, the Way of Jesus.

Romans 10:9 says, "If you confess with your mouth the Lord Jesus and believe in your heart that God has raised Him from the dead, you will be saved" (NKJV). If you have never accepted saving faith in Christ, you can pray with me right this second, wherever you are:

> Jesus, I believe in You. I believe You love me so much You came to rescue me from sin, evil, and death by Your death on the cross and to bring me new, abundant life through Your resurrection. I confess my need for a Savior and ask You to become the Lord of my life. I receive the gift of the Holy Spirit. Teach me to trust Your Word and Your guidance, direction, and instructions in my life, and give me **Crazy Faith** to follow every crazy word You say and every crazy way You lead. Amen.

You just took the first step into **Crazy Faith**! This will impact you *forever.* Your eternity is secure. Your name is written in the Lamb's Book of Life. But your decision isn't only for eventually—it's for right now. You now have access to God's very presence, His Holy Spirit, who is ready and waiting to guide you into abundant life.

In case you were wondering, you just experienced *saving faith.*

CRAZY WORSHIP

In our Christmas-in-July (or whenever) story, Mary and Joseph aren't the only players who get a crazy word from God. Some sheepherders get a crazy word in the form of an angel choir;

remember that? Some stargazing scholars from far to the east of Judea, maybe even as far as India, get a crazy word in the form of a never-before-seen star that appears out of nowhere in the sky to the west. They probably have some crazy worries along their crazy walk, and it's a trip that takes many months, so there is most definitely a crazy wait in there too.

What do they do after God makes a crazy way for them to get to Bethlehem? The only thing they *can* do, the only thing *we* can do when God makes a crazy way for us: express our loving gratitude to God in crazy worship. They bring their very best, their gifts fit for a king, and lay their gifts and themselves down before the Way, the Truth, and the Life.

> When they saw the star, they were filled with joy! They entered the house and saw the child with his mother, Mary, and they bowed down and worshiped him. Then they opened their treasure chests and gave him gifts of gold, frankincense, and myrrh. (Matthew 2:10–11)

When I got the keys, keys, keys to the SpiritBank Event Center, we at Transformation Church here in Tulsa and all over the world in Transformation Nation acted the fool in crazy worship for a month straight. It was the only thing we could do! Our Crazy Faith unlocked unbelievable and unforeseen blessings of resources, connections, favor, and so much more . . . and just like those wise men, we were filled with joy!

God had answered our prayer. We were blessed. Crazy worship

> **WHENEVER GOD MAKES A CRAZY WAY IN YOUR LIFE, THE PROPER RESPONSE IS CRAZY WORSHIP.**

was the proper response to God making a crazy way. Whenever God makes a crazy way in your life, the proper response is crazy worship.

Every blessing and promise and provision our God brings to you through **Crazy Faith** is intended to advance His mission of saving faith for everyone on the earth. What good are luxury cars and custom houses and designer sneakers for your kids without a lasting spiritual legacy of saving faith? What good is a high-powered job if those who work for you never learn how much God loves them? What good is a miraculous healing if you just keep living for yourself? What good is deliverance from addiction if you're not going to help others get free of those chains?

Remember the progression of **Crazy Faith**?

- We *accept* salvation through saving faith in Christ.
- We gain *access* to the Holy Spirit, our live-in guide to God's life in us.
- We take *action* in prayer and in real life to obey God's Word. Baby steps!
- We take *authority* over anything that stands in the way of God's will for our lives.
- We live in *abundance,* a pipeline of blessing to everyone around us.

Why? So that every single person we touch with our lives can experience saving faith in Jesus Christ and begin her own progression of faith.

Crazy Faith is like a wave: it just keeps coming . . . and coming . . . and coming.

DON'T TAKE YOUR FOOT OFF THE GAS

Together we've walked in these pages through baby, maybe, waiting, wavy, lazy, trading, fugazi, stating, fading, and saving faith—all on our way to living in **Crazy Faith**. But that's not the end. Once you begin to experience God's promise and provision in your family, your career, your neighborhood, your physical health, and so much more and begin to live in abundance and purpose in the wave of **Crazy Faith** . . . *don't stop.* Keep your foot on the gas.

When Transformation Church moved into the SpiritBank Event Center, that wasn't the end of the story. God promised us a building, but He wanted us to take the whole block. The SBEC sits at the back of a seven-building commercial complex that is home to thirty-five businesses that include a university, a military recruiting facility, chiropractic offices, salons, and restaurants. One day not long after we moved in, I was pulling into the parking lot and God whispered, *Don't take your foot off the gas. Believe Me for the whole thing.*

I had a choice in that moment to be comfortable in what my **Crazy Faith** *had* produced or to begin the maybe, waiting, wavy, active, declarative process all over again, full of trust and assurance for what my **Crazy Faith** *could still* produce. I decided to put my weight on God's whisper and believe that Transformation Church could own and manage the whole complex for God's glory.

One year and two months after we walked into our promise, I got the keys, keys, keys again.

Now to Him who is able to do exceedingly abundantly above all that we ask or think, according to the power that works in us, to Him be glory in the church by Christ Jesus to all generations, forever and ever. Amen. (Ephesians 3:20–21, NKJV)

Welcome to your new normal. This is how it's supposed to be! God isn't interested in blessing you once; He's intent on opening His floodgates to pour down continually, confirming again and again for people ready to abandon hope that *He is real.*

When they all say it's impossible, when the calculations are improbable, when the mountain seems too high, when everything looks just plain crazy . . . you look them straight in the eye, with your head up and shoulders back, and declare this:

"It's only crazy until it happens."

STATING FAITH SCRIPTURES

Afraid Ps. 34:4; Matt. 10:28; 2 Tim. 1:7; Heb. 13:5–6

Anxious Ps. 46; Matt. 6:19–34; Phil. 4:6; 1 Pet. 5:6–7

Backsliding Ps. 51; 1 John 1:4–9

Bereaved Matt. 5:4; 2 Cor. 1:3–4

Bitter or critical 1 Cor. 13

Conscious of sin Prov. 28:13

Defeated Rom. 8:31–39

Depressed Ps. 34

Disaster threatens Ps. 91; Ps. 118:5–6; Luke 8:22–25

Discouraged Ps. 23; Ps. 42:6–11; Ps. 55:22; Matt. 5:11–12;
    2 Cor. 4:8–18; Phil. 4:4–7

Doubting Matt. 8:26; Heb. 11

Facing a crisis Ps. 121; Matt. 6:25–34; Heb. 4:16

Faith fails Ps. 42:5; Heb. 11

Friends fail Ps. 41:9–13; Luke 17:3–4; Rom. 12:14, 17, 19,
    21; 2 Tim. 4:16–18

In trouble Ps. 16; Ps. 31; John 14:1–4; Heb. 7:25

Leaving home Ps. 121; Matt. 10:16–20

Lonely Ps. 23; Heb. 13:5–6

Needing God's protection Ps. 27:1–6; Ps. 91; Phil. 4:19

Needing guidance Ps. 32:8; Prov. 3:5–6

Needing peace John 14:1–4; John 16:33; Rom. 5:1–5; Phil. 4:6–7

Needing rules for living Rom. 12

Overcome Ps. 6; Rom. 8:31–39; 1 John 1:4–9

Prayerful Ps. 4; Ps. 42; Luke 11:1–13; John 17; 1 John 5:14–15

Protected Ps. 18:1–3; Ps. 34:7

Sick or in pain Jer. 17:14; Matt. 26:39; Rom. 5:3–5; 2 Cor. 12:9–10; 1 Pet. 4:12–13, 19

Sorrowful Ps. 51; Matt. 5:4; John 14; 2 Cor. 1:3–4; 1 Thess. 4:13–18

Tempted Ps. 1; Ps. 139:23–24; Matt. 26:41; 1 Cor. 10:12–14; Phil. 4:8

Thankful Ps. 100; 1 Thess. 5:18; Heb. 13:15

Traveling Ps. 121

Weary Ps. 90; Matt. 11:28–30; 1 Cor. 15:58; Gal. 6:9–10

Worried Matt. 6:19–34; 1 Pet. 5:6–7

H.O.T. QUESTIONS FOR REFLECTION

---

1. IT'S ONLY CRAZY UNTIL IT HAPPENS

- Look over your faith-foundations self-assessment (p. 10–11), then identify the area of your life with the strongest, sturdiest foundation and the area with the weakest. Explore your experiences as a child, teen, or adult that have helped to form the strong area and the weak area.

- You can dig deeper faith foundations in every area of your life, but these two—the strongest and weakest—are both good places to start (the strongest because it may feel comparatively easy to trust God for something crazy and the weakest because it will definitely *not* be easy). Pay special attention to God's prompting and direction in these two areas as you progress through the book. Whom will you ask to pray specifically about these areas of your life as you make this 𝕮𝖗𝖆𝖟𝖞 𝕱𝖆𝖎𝖙𝖍 journey?

- **Daily Faith:** Memorize Jesus's words recorded in John 15:16, "You didn't choose me. I chose you. I appointed you to go and produce lasting fruit, so that the Father will give you whatever you ask for, using my name." If and when you feel unworthy, doubtful, anxious, impatient, unmotivated, or overwhelmed this week, let the Holy Spirit remind you of this promise about your purpose. You are not a mistake! You are chosen.

2. BABY FAITH

- What is something in your life that's hard for you to believe God cares about? In your journal or in conversation with a friend, investigate the reason(s) why. Do you feel embarrassed? Ashamed? Silly? Immature? Or could it be that your idea of God is too distant or removed from your everyday life? Or that you find it hard to really believe He truly loves you? (Or maybe all of the above?)

- Consider the area of your life that you identified as having the weakest faith foundation. What is one baby step of faith you can take to strengthen the rudiments, the fundamentals, in this area? Whom will you ask to pray with you for hope and courage to imagine what God wants to do in, for, and through you?

- **Daily Faith:** Memorize Jesus's words in John 15:9, "I have loved you even as the Father has loved me. Remain in my love." This week, practice remaining in Jesus's love. If and when you hear whispers in your mind that cast doubt on His love for you, speak His words aloud and push your faith roots deeper. Refuse to be moved. Remain.

3. MAYBE FAITH

- "Stepping out in faith will make you leave what's familiar for what's uncomfortable. . . . God wants to meet you at the intersection of faith and obedience" (p. 59). Taking even the itty-bittiest baby step can be scary when you're not 100 percent sure everything will turn out exactly the way you hope. As you consider the vision God has placed in your heart, try to quantify your assurance. Do you have 16 percent faith? 43 percent? What kind of encouragement, prophetic word, or testimony could help tip you over the 51 percent mark? Who in your community could help you gain that assurance?

· You may intellectually agree that God is trustworthy, but actually trusting Him means putting your weight on His word. What action do you need to take to put more of your weight on Him? Who can help keep you accountable and encouraged as you act in faith?

· **Daily Faith:** Memorize Jesus's last words spoken from the cross, recorded in Luke 23:46, "Father, I entrust my spirit into your hands!" Any time you are uncertain about trusting God's purpose and plan, pray these words aloud along with Jesus.

4. WAITING FAITH

· Where do you see pressure, comparison, discontentment, or impatience driving you toward FOMO? Take some time to examine what's behind your fear. Write down some specific strategies for choosing waiting faith over hasty faith.

· Are you wasting your wait? "God sometimes tests our patience to build our endurance, train us to handle what's coming, and teach us to trust fully in Him" (p. 73). As you wait on the provision of God's promise, how will you wait on (serve!) Him? Who in your faith community or circle of friends needs support for their vision? How will you allow sacrificial service to shape you for God's purpose? Be specific and accountable to someone on the 𝕮𝖗𝖆𝖟𝖞 𝕱𝖆𝖎𝖙𝖍 journey with you.

- **Daily Faith:** Memorize Jesus's words in John 15:8, "When you produce much fruit, you are my true disciples. This brings great glory to my Father." If and when you get that FOMO feeling, an urgency to make something happen out of God's timing, claim this promise aloud. You can continue to produce fruit by serving God and others while you wait for His provision.

5. WAVY FAITH

- Reflect on a time when you were in troubling, confusing, frustrating, or painful circumstances—and only later realized how God used that situation for your benefit and for the benefit of others. How might your present stormy circumstances be a part of His provision and purpose for you? Use your imagination!

- How is God prompting you to get out of your safety zone and meet Him on the waves? What daily spiritual discipline will you keep this week to practice drawing close to Him? (Fasting? Scripture meditation? WAVY prayer?) Who can help keep you accountable to your practice?

- **Daily Faith:** Memorize Matthew 14:28–29, "Then Peter called to him, 'Lord, if it's really you, tell me to come to you, walking on the water.' 'Yes, come,' Jesus said." As you commit it to memory in mind and heart, practice saying yes to Jesus.

6. LAZY FAITH

- Be honest with yourself and your 𝕮𝖗𝖆𝖟𝖞 𝕱𝖆𝖎𝖙𝖍 community: In what area of your faith life are you feeling laziest and least motivated? What kind of prophetic work do you need to undertake to get going? To do something you haven't yet? To *stop* doing something that's prohibiting your growth in God? Whom will you ask to partner with you in accountability so you get moving in active faith?

- Consider your *why*. Write it down. Where are you in the process of realigning your *why* with God's? How will you seek His divine help to surrender your *why* to Him?

- **Daily Faith:** Memorize Philippians 2:13, "God is working in you, giving you the desire and the power to do what pleases him." If and when lazy faith rears its head and yawns, speak aloud this promise. You're not acting on your own; God is ready and willing to give you everything you need to please Him!

7. TRADING FAITH

- Reflect on and express gratitude for how the faith of others brought you closer to Jesus. Who prayed for you when you couldn't pray? Who met your needs when you were hopeless? Who encouraged you to be faithful when you were ready to give up? If you haven't taken time to thank them, do it! Otherwise they may never know how their active faith produced fruit in your life.

- What is your mat, your testimony? How has Christ made you free? How can sharing your testimony help you defeat the Enemy's attacks on you and others?

- **Daily Faith:** Read and reflect on Psalm 139:13–18, then memorize verse 14, "Thank you for making me so wonderfully complex! Your workmanship is marvelous—how well I know it." What makes you different from everyone else? How is God working uniquely in your exceptional life? If and when you feel trapped by your past or others' doubts, give thanks with the psalmist that you are the exception!

8. FUGAZI FAITH

- Christian faith is supposed to start with acceptance of Christ as Savior and Lord and then progress through access (to the Holy Spirit), action (in faithful obedience), authority (over anything that hinders our purpose), and finally to abundance and an overflow of blessing. Honestly assess where you are on the journey. What specific step(s) will you take this week to continue your progress?
- "God will do everything we can't do but nothing that we can" (p. 153). Where is your faith incomplete because you're waiting for God or someone else to do the work of love? What fear, bitterness, emotional wound, stubbornness, or sense of entitlement is keeping you from your work? Whom will you ask for support, encouragement, and accountability?
- **Daily Faith:** Memorize 1 Corinthians 13:13, "Three things will last forever—faith, hope, and love—and the greatest of these is love." If and when your faith starts to feel fake, like you're just going through the motions, speak this verse aloud and reorient yourself to work that will last for eternity. Let faith be made complete in you!

9. STATING FAITH

- When you practice the faith-filled declarations exercise (p. 164), how do you feel? Encouraged? Awkward? Foolish? Empowered? (All of the above?) Why?
- Where in your life are you experiencing the Enemy's suggestions? Don't keep it to yourself! Invite a friend or group of friends into this journey so they can state faith along with you. And as others share their worries, doubts, confusion, and disappointments with you, tell them (out loud!) where you see God at work in, for, and through them.
- **Daily Faith:** Choose one "Stating Faith Scripture" (p. 171–74) to memorize this week. When the Enemy whispers to your mind, declare what is true from God's Word.

10. FADING FAITH

- If you are experiencing fading faith, what loss, failure, or disappointment is at the root? If you haven't told anyone else yet, find a trustworthy friend to share with. Thomas stayed with the other disciples even when he was still waiting for his miracle. Don't suffer fading faith alone.
- What tangible, visual, and personal needs can God meet through your community to sustain your faith? What feelings or fears are keeping you from asking others to share your burdens?
- **Daily Faith:** Memorize Galatians 6:2, "Share each other's burdens, and in this way obey the law of Christ." Remind yourself and others that you're in the Way of Christ together, that no one walks alone.

11. SAVING FAITH

- What crazy word have you received from God? Write it down, and share it with others.
- What crazy worry keeps coming up in your mind and heart? Share it with others, and pray about it. All of it.
- What is the next step in your crazy walk? What encouragement, challenge, support, or accountability do you need to get going? Ask for it.
- What are you doing to wait on (serve!) God and others during your crazy wait? Keep track of how God is growing and shaping you to become who He wants you to be as you wait on Him.
- What crazy way is God making for you? If you can't see it yet, that's okay. God always brings new life out of our crap when we turn to Jesus.
- Even if His crazy way for you is still developing, get in the habit of crazy worship. When you worship, you point others to the Author and Giver of Life who stands ready to save anyone who has 𝕮𝖗𝖆𝖟𝖞 𝕱𝖆𝖎𝖙𝖍 to believe.
- **Daily Faith:** Memorize Galatians 6:9, "Let's not get tired of doing what is good. At just the right time we will reap a harvest of blessing if we don't give up."

ACKNOWLEDGMENTS

Every accomplishment in my life has been supported in love and prayer by some very important people, and this is no exception. I have been blessed to be surrounded by a host of people that uplift, execute, and believe in the vision that God has given to me. I would like to take this time to acknowledge my community, my team, and my family.

To my wife and so much more, Natalie Diane Todd, your love for me is inconceivable. Thank you for never giving up on me through my deficiencies, insecurity, and immaturity. Your prayers, grace, and patience allowed me to grow into the man I am today. Thank you for our children, Isabella, Michael Jr., Ava, and Gia; they bring so much bliss into my life. You affirm me and encourage me; you push me beyond my comprehension of success. You will forever be my partner, my passion, and my purpose.

To my parents, Tommy a.k.a. "The Captain" and Brenda Todd, thank you for your abounding wisdom and relentless belief in me. Your encouragement, prayers, and example of faith have shaped me into the man I am today. Thank you for showing me how to lead my family with unconditional love, abundant grace, and strength. Thank you for being the greatest depiction of our heavenly Father's love here on this earth.

To Bishop Gary and Pastor Debbie McIntosh, your 𝕮𝖗𝖆𝖟𝖞 𝕱𝖆𝖎𝖙𝖍 to start a church and CRAZIER FAITH to hand it to me has proved to be God. Thank you for believing in my leadership when I didn't know how. Thank you for keeping your word to stand with me after the leadership transition. I can always count on an encouraging text or a strong "Amen" every week. You don't know how that fuels my faith and models how to transition well.

To Brie and Aaron Davis, the friends turned sister and brother I never knew I needed, thank you for always being right by my side. Thank you for your persistent authenticity in our friendship. Through every failed project and successful venture, you both have remained a consistent support system. And—thank you for letting me use your house as my personal "book-writing office."

To Charles Metcalf, one of my best friends, a creative samurai, and sermon-execution specialist. Thank you for listening to all my crazy ideas and believing in them at first mention. You give me the space to dream and see visions that are bigger than our current borders. I feel safe trusting you with the raw, unedited, unpolished versions of me, and I pray that every leader gets a Charles Metcalf.

To Jonathan Vinnett, thank you for illustrating the visions of my heart with such clarity. For years, you have made my words come to life and illuminated the ideas that I couldn't adequately articulate. Your ability to see beyond the tangible has afforded me the privilege to create in the confidence that my vision would be accurately interpreted to the world. Thank you for growing with me on this ever-evolving journey of creativity.

To Alex Field, my literary agent, thank you for playing an instrumental role in making this dream come true. Thank you for your guidance, support, and confidence in the process of this project. You've been by my side every step of the way, sharing your wisdom, giving guidance, and lending encouragement whenever necessary. Thank you for believing in the vision that was given to me. Thank you for believing in me.

To Melody Dunlap (my God-sister) and Aly Hawkins, thank you for your many contributions to this project. In a great way, without you this would not be possible. Your competence in the literary sphere has ensured that this book would be created and interpreted in excellence. Thank you for taking the time to share this experience with me and making it one I will never forget.

To the team at WaterBrook, thank you for your commitment to the execution and completion of this project. The joy, excitement, and energy that you all brought made this an unforgettably enjoyable experience. Your attention to detail and focus on even the small things left me confident that I was working with the right team. All of your hard work and efforts are very much appreciated.

To Transformation Church and TC Nation, this is for you! Thank you for your love, support, and prayers for me and my family. The relentless affection that I feel from you motivates me to continue the fulfillment of my purpose. To the TC staff, thank you all for your continued dedication and commitment to the vision and partners of TC. Thank you for allowing me to represent God outside the walls of our church. I'm humbled and honored to be your leader.

ABOUT THE AUTHOR

MICHAEL TODD is the lead pastor of Transformation Church in Tulsa, Oklahoma, alongside his wife, Natalie. They were entrusted with Transformation Church from the founding pastor, Bishop Gary McIntosh, in 2015, after fifteen years of operation.

Their personal philosophy and driving passion at Transformation Church is re-presenting God to the lost and found for transformation in Christ. They aspire to reach their community, city, and world with the gospel presented in a relevant and progressive way. The fast-growing church publishes a magazine called *Transpire;* produces their own worship music, Transformation Worship; and hosted the first Transformation Conference in 2019. You can find out more details about Transformation Church at www.transformchurch.us.

In addition, Michael has spoken at a variety of influential churches, events, universities, and conferences, including Elevation Church (Steven Furtick), C3 Conference (Fellowship Church), Lakewood Church (Joel Osteen), VOUS Conference (VOUS Church), Relentless Church (John Gray), XO Marriage Conference (Gateway Church), and others.

Michael and Natalie have been married since 2010 and live in Tulsa with four beautiful children—their daughters, Isabella, Ava, and Gia, and their son, Michael Jr.

You can contact Michael in any of these ways:

@iammiketodd
www.iammiketodd.com

Did *Crazy Faith* move you?
Challenge you?
Motivate you?

Share your thoughts with Pastor Mike about how *Crazy Faith* inspired you at IAmMikeTodd.com/CrazyFaithStories

WATERBROOK

IAmMikeTodd.com/CrazyFaithStories

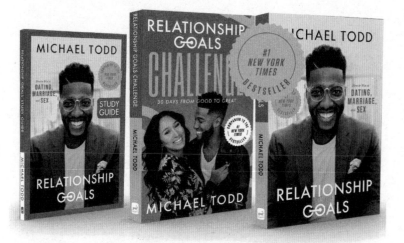

WHAT READERS ARE SAYING ABOUT *RELATIONSHIP GOALS*

★ ★ ★ ★ ★

"A great God-centered read."

★ ★ ★ ★ ★

"Chapters 8 and 9 are worth the buy . . ."

★ ★ ★ ★ ★

"A H.O.T. book (HONEST, OPEN, and TRANSPARENT)."

★ ★ ★ ★ ★

"Progress, not perfection."

★ ★ ★ ★ ★

"Get. This. Book."

DAMAGED BUT NOT DESTROYED

by

Michael Todd

COMING
FALL 2023

WATERBROOK